T0267203

The Kilgore sisters and cousins: *left to right*, Cousin Junior and dog Tippy (mother of Jack), Aileen, Mary Alice, Cousin Mary Lee, Francys, and Jane

WHEN THE WOLF CAMPED AT OUR DOOR

My Childhood in the Great Depression

Aileen Kilgore Henderson

The University of Alabama Press   Tuscaloosa

The University of Alabama Press
Tuscaloosa, Alabama 35487-0380
uapress.ua.edu

Typeface: Scala Pro

Cover images: Courtesy of Aileen Kilgore Henderson
Cover design: Michele Myatt Quinn

Cataloging-in-Publication data is available from the Library
of Congress.
ISBN: 978-0-8173-2133-8
E-ISBN: 978-0-8173-9413-4

To my readers who have encouraged me through all these years. Thank you!

Contents

WHEN THE
WOLF CAMPED
AT OUR DOOR

Introduction

THERE WERE SIX OF US living in the farmhouse as the Great Depression tightened its grip on the world: Daddy, Mama, Francys, Jane, Mary Alice, and me, Aileen. In the gloom of December 1932 my brother Buddy was born.

Our settlement of Brookwood, Alabama, stretched one building deep along the gravel highway connecting Tuscaloosa (17 miles west) to Birmingham (45 miles northeast). The center of life was the new school and, across the highway from it, Mr. Martz's orange-painted store. Several houses clustered around the store.

After Daddy lost his job at the mines in 1928, we had no steady income. Winters were unusually cold, summers hot and dry. Crops couldn't grow well, and food was scarce. Mama oversaw the garden and parceled out our meals, of necessity deaf to our complaints about cornbread in a glass of buttermilk every night for supper, with fried tripe for variety once in a while.

Shoes were in short supply, and the few clothes we had were all hand-me-downs. We children were not proud: the arrival of a box of clothes from kinfolks up north filled us with excitement for weeks. Mary Alice wore Aunt Martha's high-heeled sandals to walk up the Birmingham Highway to school, her toes red from the frost, while Francys wrapped up in a cousin's old army overcoat, a relic from his service in World War I, or "the 1918 war" as we called it then. When I was sixth-grade valedictorian and had to give a speech in the school auditorium to students and parents, Mama remade a green chiffon dress from Aunt Martha in Pittsburgh to fit my skinny body and I hid my bare feet under a table. Mama bought remnants at Brown's Bargain Basement to make my older sisters the occasional blouse, using the leftover scraps for piecing quilts to keep us warm in winter.

Sometimes Mama made us use folded bedspreads for shawls when we walked to school. We were embarrassed to be seen wearing bedspreads, but that wind we walked into was right off the icy Appalachian foothills. We wished we could join the Black children, who were waiting around a campfire for their school bus. We knew they would have invited us to warm ourselves, but they were on the road that went south toward their school, and we had to walk east to ours. We did not wonder why this was, that they went to a different school from us. To our childhood minds it was just the way the grown folks ran the world.

School was the bright spot in our lives. But school was one of the first joys we lost. The county ran out of money to pay the teachers and the schools had to close for a while.

Despite all this, I thought life was full of hope. I longed to hold on to it, so I scribbled down daily events on whatever odds and ends of paper I could find and drew pictures to illustrate our lives in a big book with blank pages that Daddy got for me.

In a magazine that relatives brought us I found the poem to go with my diary:

> *The wolf keeps camping at our door;*
> *he looks just like an apparition.*
> *Alas, alack! We are so poor,*
> *he's bound to die of malnutrition.*

After Daddy read the poem, he said, "The wolf's not just camping at our door. He's rattling the doorknob and blowing his hot breath through the keyhole."

Our situation was typical of many families in the rural South during the Great Depression. We lived in a small community made up of whatever houses were within walking distance of each other, whose residents rarely had access to radio, newspapers, or telephones. As in most similar communities then, no outside authority was available for us to turn to in situations of need or injustice not covered by the law. We had to muddle along on our own as best we could.

As you read these stories, think about what you would have done in each circumstance, given the limitations of time, place, and class. Would you drink "white dog tea" if you believed it would cure your sickness? Could you have determined which side of Mr. Prude's character was the true one—the "precious papa" or the man who wouldn't give his mother a deathbed promise, even when threatened with her restless spirit? If you had been along on the trip to see the sword in the tree, would you have let people believe a pretty story to help them through hard times or told them the truth? What was the real reason for the Ku Klux Klan's visit to Big Hurricane Baptist—were they trying to intimidate someone? Would you have thrown their money in the outhouse as Brother Hutton urged? And how hungry would you have to be to eat wormy cabbage?

In this collection of true stories spotlighting my growing-up years of the 1930s, we children contended with illness, death, homelessness, old age, and unnamed horrors. Join with my family in the telling of stories on the grassy lawn after supper, stories that united us as a family not only with each other but with our ancestors and our descendants.

1

Oscar Meets an Ottomobeel

DURING WINTER DAYS ON THE farm, most nights after supper we gathered close to the small grate in our living room. Daddy would bring his precious metal box of mementos out of the closet and we'd follow him into the past. He remembered each piece of battered jewelry and told us about the person it had belonged to. No sparkling stones remained in any of the settings. They had been removed and sold or traded during the constant hard times. But Daddy told us of his plans to reset the stones and restore the gold plate "when his ship came in," as it surely would. We dreamed with him while Mama sat in the background mending our clothes and saying nothing.

"This is a pin Grandma Jane Luther brought with her from England when she was a girl. And Grandpa Morris gave her this one when they married," he'd say, holding up each piece in turn. One piece that always made us sad was a small gold ring.

"This was my little sister Nettie's," Daddy said. "She got it for her last birthday when she was three." Oscar, our daddy, and Nettie had the same birthday—January 22—and they celebrated together.

"Mother always saved up to make us a special cake and we had a family celebration wherever we lived," Daddy said. "But that spring when Nettie took sick, nothing helped her." He silently turned the ring in his fingers. Then he said, "My birthdays were never the same after Nettie died."

At times like this to cheer us up, we'd ask Daddy for a story from the four years that his family lived in the neglected Prude house at the turn of the century. Built before the Civil War, it was haunted, which made it even more interesting to Oscar and his brother Davis. The day the family moved into the house the weather was dreary and rainy. The movers had heard about the haints and evil happenings in the long-vacant house and were in a hurry to be finished and gone. While they were unloading the family piano from the wagon, one of the children came running from under the house hollering, "A lion! A baby lion alive!" The men let go of the piano and grabbed planks and sticks to kill the monster. What they found in the basement was an enormous old rooster, standing on one foot, all drawn up, wet and sick. They threw down their weapons and returned to salvage the muddy, battered piano.

More unsettling than that, however, were the dark nights the boys lay awake listening to the long-dead Mr. Prude tap-tap-tapping along the hall with his walking stick. They dared not say a word when Mr. Prude's uncertain steps hesitated at their door, but in the silence Oscar nudged Davis and Davis nudged Oscar while they held their breaths until the old man resumed his tap-tap-tapping toward the back door. That way led toward the cedar tree where the pot of money was buried.

The boys knew all about that pot of money. It was meant for their grandfather who was orphaned by the Civil War and raised by the Prudes. Oscar and Davis kept a shovel handy so they could dig for the treasure during any spare moment they had. They were handicapped by having just one shovel. While one boy shoveled, the other one took a rest, and they talked about how they'd spend the treasure.

Davis set his mind on buying a ticket on the train west to become a cowboy. Oscar couldn't decide. He considered buying the Cottondale store so he could have whatever he wanted whenever he wanted it. Uncle Giles said, "Buy an ottomobeel! That's the thing." And Giles sang while fiddling a square dance tune, "Bee-la-bill, going uphill, kicking up dust like an ottomobeel."

But Oscar knew how dangerous those newfangled machines were: if an ottomobeel wanted to leave the road and come after you, it could chase you down and run over you. Besides that, if it didn't want to work for you, it would just blow up and kill you.

One day their mother asked the boys to go to the store in Cottondale to get cornmeal to make mush for supper. Brother Davis said, "I went last time," and he disappeared. So off Oscar went along Keene's Mill Road never dreaming that this was the day he'd meet an ottomobeel. Ox-drawn wagons, yes, or a horse and buggy, perhaps. But an infernal combustion engine? Never. They cost too much, and who in Cottondale had the understanding to drive one of them?

Oscar didn't mind going to the store. This was a chance to add to his arrowhead collection. He usually found them in ditches where the earth had been disturbed. He kept every one, broken or whole. This was a good day for finding arrowheads, and he became so interested in his search that at first he didn't hear anything out of the ordinary. But suddenly he stopped in his tracks, ears alert. Put-put-put-put-putting. A sound like he'd never heard before. Coming toward him—fast. Just around the curve and out of sight. Oscar's heart almost leaped out of his body. It had to be one of those ottomobeels!

Climb a tree! his mind ordered. There wasn't a tree.

Get in a cave! No caves anywhere.

Yonder! A big stump! Up the incline overlooking the road! From behind the stump he could see but not be seen. Crouching there, heart pounding, hardly breathing, he vowed he'd risk his life to see this thing.

His ears roared so loud he could hardly hear as it came in sight. He blinked his eyes to see it clearer: a bare-bones chunk of machinery with smoke boiling out its back end and a rattling racket coming out the front end.

A man perched under a guiding bar was fighting to hold the thing on the road while it bucked and kicked, trying to get away. The goggles the man wore and the kerchief knotted around his long neck made him look like a praying mantis, and a white duster flapped around his knees.

Oscar kept perfectly still. He didn't want that wild machine to notice him. He was still trembling after it raced past and vanished around the curve. When he could no longer hear it, he sighed and gathered strength to stand. At first his legs would not hold him up, but as soon as he was able he started toward Cottondale again.

An ottomobeel! And he'd lived to tell Davis about it! He couldn't keep from skipping in excitement though skipping was something only girls did.

On the way home, holding tight to his small sack of cornmeal, Oscar looked for the thing's tracks. It was like following a snake's tracks only a whole lot easier. During the three-mile hike, he never once thought of looking for arrowheads. And when he got home, oh, how envious Davis was that he had missed seeing what Oscar had seen.

But something was wrong with Oscar. At first he didn't realize what had happened to his thinking. He just knew that he couldn't forget that ottomobeel. It turned out that his problem was he had moved from the horse-and-buggy era into the machine age. How dandy it would be to speed along the road honking his horn, scattering everybody in his path—cats and dogs, chickens and people—and kicking dust in their eyes. When folks heard him coming, they'd run out of their houses to watch him pass, and boys would climb trees or hide. And he, Oscar, would blast his horn while he waved and laughed. Then, before he drove out of sight, he'd make the machine kick up its hind wheels and backfire.

Then he thought how he could make another fortune charging people to ride in his ottomobeel! He'd be a millionaire in no time. All he needed was to locate that treasure.

"But Davis and I finally woke up to reality," Daddy told us. "We had worn our digging shovel down to a nub and we had no money to buy a new one."

"Didn't you ever find the treasure?" little Mary Alice asked anxiously.

"No," said Daddy. "It's still there. It's waiting for one of you to find it."

And we all grinned at the possibility.

2

Alma's Dime

As soon as I woke up that spring day, I put on my shirt and overalls and padded into the kitchen to look at the calendar. April 10, 1931. My birthday! Ten years old! A decade, Daddy had said. Mama was in the barn milking but she had already baked my birthday cake—a pound cake—for midday dinner. The kitchen smelled of vanilla and almond flavorings. My mouth watered as I looked at that golden cake cooling on the table. It was hard to resist pinching a bit out of its crusty brown side, but that would spoil its perfection, not to mention get me in trouble.

The passing day just kept getting better and better. My sister Francys said she'd do dishes in my place, and Mama said I could have the afternoon off to go play with Alma and her gang of brothers and sisters.

I didn't waste any time. After washing my face, I combed my hair and stuffed my shirttail into my overalls.

"You need a dress to wear on special days like this," Mama said, watching me. "I could make you one in no time if I just had two feed sacks that matched."

"If I wore a dress, I'd have to have shoes," I reminded her.

"You'll have a dress—two of them—and shoes too," Daddy said, "if this depression ever gets over."

"I don't want a dress or shoes," I said. "I like having lots of pockets in my overalls and going barefooted."

I reached under my side of the bed for the sack of paper dolls I cut out of last year's Sears and Roebuck catalog. There was a chance Alma might want to play paper dolls. Then I went skipping down our lane.

Racing along the gravel road that wound toward the Brookwood store, I looked ahead toward the fence corner where the path turned into the woods. That was the only part I dreaded—those deep shadows, the creepy birdcalls, and even a different kind of smell. But what did I see ahead? Yonder came Alma from the store. We'd just about meet at the corner. I wouldn't have to go through the woods by myself!

I waved my sack of paper dolls and she waved back with her fist. I could tell she was grinning like a possum and I found out why when we got in hollering distance.

"You'll never guess what I found," she beamed.

"What? What?" I asked, hurrying toward her. "A penny? A diamond ring?"

She opened her fist. A dime! Better than a penny! Better than a diamond ring!

"You know the bench where the men always sit?" she asked. "Wasn't nobody sittin' there now so I could look under it. And right away I saw the dime winking at me! Ten whole cents!"

"Yeah!" I said. "Think what that'll buy." A loaf of bread for one thing but I didn't want her to remember anything so practical. "Ten Baby Ruths! Twenty oatmeal cookies! Two packs of teaberry gum! Come on, I'll go back with you." I never doubted she would share.

She closed her hand tight over the dime and drew back. "No, no. I ain't going to spend it. I'm going to Aunt Susie."

"What for? You got no use for her—she just births babies. Come on back to the store." I grabbed her arm and tried to turn her around.

She stood firm, planted. "I'm going to get my fortune told."

"What you want to know your fortune for? Besides, Aunt Susie's a seer. That's the devil's work. Besides, I'm gonna tell the preacher. He'll make you stand up in church and confess. Besides . . ." I really never had thought of all this but I saw that dime escaping from me. "And besides it's too far to the Quarters."

The few Black people in our part of Brookwood lived in the small houses left from the once-large farm beyond our farm. We knew all of them, especially Aunt Janie and her husband Mr. Will, Aunt Susie,

Julia, Roy Morgan (Mama hired him and his mule to help her in our garden), Lewis (who helped us at pig-killing time), and a couple of others.

Alma pulled loose from me and started off. Nothing else to do but follow her. Maybe Aunt Susie wouldn't be at home. Maybe one of her wild dogs would scare Alma away.

We trotted past my house, past Shag's house, past Rozelle's. He was playing in the yard and I waved, still trying to think of a way to keep that dime from being wasted.

Alma tore through the cotton patch without a glance at the white and pink blossoms everywhere, looking just like the hollyhocks in our yard. We whizzed past Aunt Janie's house. Mr. Will's hauling wagon was parked in the shade of a persimmon tree. Nearby slouched his ox team half-asleep, chewing their cuds.

I was tired of trotting. "Slow down," I panted. "I'm not going to take that dime away from you. And Aunt Susie won't go anywhere. If she can tell fortunes, then she knows you're coming."

None of Aunt Susie's dogs were in sight, worse luck. At the steps, Alma paused and wiped her red face with her skirt. Then she set her jaw and went up on the porch to knock.

The door opened so fast that I knew Aunt Susie had seen us coming. "What you young'uns want? Is somebody sick?" I could barely see her. She was as dark as the room behind her.

"I want my fortune told," Alma said, showing the dime.

Aunt Susie inched back the door. I made ready to squeeze through with Alma but Aunt Susie's bulk blocked me, and I was shut out. I heard the latch click.

What a disgusting setback! I plopped myself down on the edge of the porch, swinging my dusty, ant-bitten feet. I couldn't even hear voices. How long was a dime's worth of fortune? I took out my paper dolls and arranged them into families. They were all so good-looking and well dressed, even the children, that I liked to study them and change them around. It seemed like hours before the latch clicked again and the door cracked open. Alma slipped out and without a word took off in a hurry. She was almost out of sight before I could get my paper dolls back in the sack and catch up.

"What'd she say?" I demanded. "What's going to happen to you? You gonna marry that Grubb Tubbs or what?"

Her eyes were on the ground. She didn't answer.

"You dragged me way off over here—you coulda at least let me come in. What'd she say?"

"Nothin'. Just nothin'."

"Then you've still got the dime. We can go to the store."

"Nope. No dime. No store. I got to go home and help with the night work."

"You mean you don't have a future? Are you fixing to die?"

"None of your business," she said mean-like.

Neither of us spoke again on the way home. When we parted at my lane I watched, getting madder and madder, while she hurried to the fence corner. Before she turned and disappeared in the woods, I cupped my hands around my mouth and bellowed my anger.

"Ten Baby Ruths woulda made you a whole lot happier!"

At least, I admitted to myself, only two Baby Ruths would have made *me* happier on my one and only tenth birthday!

3

Friends Again

ON A COLD NIGHT IN November 1931 as we finished our supper Mama said, "What a lot of leftovers. Maybe we should send them to Alma's family. Aileen, you and Mary Alice could take them."

I stiffened. "Mama, you know Alma and I aren't friends anymore."

"That's foolishness—I suspect neither one of you remembers why you're mad."

"She tore up my sandcastle village I was building at the spring," I said, getting mad all over again.

"You don't know that it was Alma," Jane pointed out.

"I *know* it was Alma 'cause it happened right after she found that dime and wasted it having her fortune told. I wanted her to buy Baby Ruths."

"But wasn't it her dime?" Jane asked.

I wasn't listening. I was old enough to realize it wasn't just Alma I was mad about. We hadn't seen my daddy in a month, four whole weeks, and he'd just written us from a place called Marked Tree, Arkansas, to say the railroad was sending him next to Pensacola, Florida, probably to work till after Christmas. In all my life we'd never celebrated Christmas without him. Since he left in October he'd ridden the train to work at Tupelo in Mississippi, Memphis in Tennessee, and Cordova, Boligee, and Linden, all in Alabama. And now Arkansas and Florida after that. We were glad for the money—Mama could buy food for us, pay our overdue grocery bills, our mortgage so we wouldn't be turned out of our farm, our school fees, and lots of other things that put gray in Daddy's hair and a worried frown on Mama's face.

I didn't stop to consider these things now. I just knew that ole Alma Booth could starve for all I cared, but it wouldn't do to say that.

"It's a long way over there through the woods. And it's dark," I growled.

"Alma's daddy lost his job and they have a new baby at their house. They may need food," Mama said. She was busy pouring the rest of the big butter beans into a jar with a tight lid, wrapping the remainder of the crusty cornbread in clean paper, and emptying the pitcher of buttermilk into another jar. "Francys, look in the cabinet there and get a jar of pickled peaches. They'll be a tasty ending to the Booths' supper."

"That's way too much," I complained. "We can't carry all that."

"Of course you can," Mama said. "Now wrap up tight. Wear your toboggans so you don't come home with an earache."

Before I could think of any more excuses we were out the door into the biting wind and dark. We hurried barefoot along the cold road up to the corner then turned to take the path through the woods. The only sound was the creaking of the frozen tree branches. I was in front lugging the jug of buttermilk and the still warm cornbread. Mary Alice followed with the rest of the supper. I had no trouble finding the familiar path. I recognized certain trees from the times I use to play with Alma back when we were friends.

We crossed the footlog over the little creek and started up the long sloping hill to the house. At the top of the hill we stopped under a big oak to catch our breath because we'd been traveling pretty fast. Farther ahead we saw the log house Mr. Booth had built himself. The front door stood open and there was a blazing fire in the fireplace. We knew that was the custom even on the coldest of nights. A person lost in the woods would see the fire as a beacon to a safe haven.

But what was that sound? Above the blustering of the wind and the crackling of the frozen trees we heard singing, sweet singing, like the angels. The family was singing a hymn! When they finished Mr. Booth began praying. We couldn't understand his words but we knew by his respectful tone that he was speaking to the Lord.

We started on and entered the yard just as they all said, "Amen." I hollered, "Halloooo," and Mary Alice called out, "We're here!"

Alma's daddy appeared in the door to welcome us.

"We've got some stuff here we couldn't use," I said stumbling over my words, "and Mama thought maybe y'all could use it."

We set our burdens on the bare table. The children gathered round looking bug-eyed at what we'd brought as Alma began unpacking it. I ignored Alma and she didn't look at me.

"Praise the Lord!" her father said. "You two are an answer to prayer. There's not a crumb of food in this house and the children are hungry." Tears ran down his cheeks even as he smiled at us.

"Come to the fire and warm," Alma's pale mama said, smiling her toothless smile. The fire popped and crackled and felt good on my cold hands and nose.

Trevena set down bowls, Herbert got glasses, and Alma was dividing out the supper. Their eyes never left the food. At our house we'd had some scanty meals but we'd never been that hungry.

"We need to go," I said. "It's a long way back."

"Before you leave you must see our new boy," Mr. Booth said. "He's asleep now in his cradle. Alma'll show you. She takes good care of him."

Alma drew back the cover from a red, wrinkled little creature that was as big as a minute.

"Isn't he cute?" she said to me.

I nodded but I thought, "Baby pigs are a lot cuter."

Mary Alice gently rocked the cradle. The baby stirred and yawned looking like a miniature Methuselah, the oldest man ever. Even I had to laugh at him.

By now the food was divided out. At each place sat a bowl of butter beans, with a slice of brown crusty cornbread on the side, and a glass of buttermilk. The pickled peaches looked rosy in the center of the table—enough of them for a whole sweet-tart peach for each person. Everybody except Alma was seated on the benches, waiting for us to leave so the eating could begin.

Alma took me by the arm and pulled me to the corner where her schoolbooks were stacked on a shelf.

"I've got something for you," she said reaching behind her geography book and bringing out a penny Baby Ruth. "The storekeeper paid me for sweeping his floor."

I didn't want her candy she had worked for but I knew I had to take it. "Thank you," I said. "Did you tear up my sandcastle village?"

"No, it was Huey and those boys who live over at the trestle."

On the way home, going through the dark, creaking woods, I was not afraid. I was too busy dealing with being an answer to prayer. How amazing that Mr. Booth would be praying for food even while Mama was preparing to send him some. God used Mary Alice and me to deliver the answer to his prayer. What a strange feeling! But a good feeling—and in my pocket was that penny Baby Ruth that signified Alma and I were friends again. I knew I didn't deserve it.

"I'll give it to little Buddy," I resolved to myself. "No, to Mama because she loves chocolate and she's the one who answered Mr. Booth's prayer."

4

Mama Prevents Murder

MAMA'S YOUNGEST SISTER MARTHA LIVED in Pittsburgh. Her daughter, Mary Lee, was my age but the two of us had never been friends. I was about ten when Aunt Martha wrote us that she would be coming to visit and would be bringing Mary Lee with her. I was not enthusiastic.

"She's not going to sleep with me," I announced.

"She can stay in the back bedroom with Francys and me," Jane said calmly.

"She's not even going to come upstairs," I continued. "I don't want her prying into my things."

Mary Alice shared the upstairs room with me and she didn't object. Her own affairs kept her busy. Somebody else could worry about the Yankee cousin.

I knew that Mary Lee's family was rich. I was sure she didn't even know there was a depression going on. I was the ungrateful receiver of cast-off clothes from her—fancy dresses and short-sleeved blouses—the kind of clothes I admired but didn't wear. My daily uniform was a faded pair of overalls worn with a long-sleeved white shirt and no underwear. I could get in and out of it quick, and it was good protection from black gnats, stinging nettle, and the burning sun. I could even sleep in it if Mama didn't catch me. Every Saturday Mama washed my outfit while I stayed in bed in my nightshirt reading or drawing until it dried.

Even after the visitors arrived we continued our daily routine: each morning after Mama finished her chores and before she started mid-day dinner, she sat down in a rocker to catch her breath. At that time I always combed her long, dark-brown hair and braided it. Aunt Martha would pull up a rocker and sit with Mama while they talked about their growing up. Their mother had run the only hotel in their small town with the help of her daughters.

"We Cox girls were known as the belles of Pickensville," Aunt Martha said, laughing. "And how beautifully you could dance, Gertrude! I remember everybody stopped dancing just to watch you and your partner."

My mama dance? We were strict Baptists—no dancing allowed. Dancing was cause for being turned out of the church. I noticed that Mama made no comment. I learned other things too that amazed me, about drummers, or salesmen, and gamblers who came in on the Tombigbee River boats, and about people who sneaked out of town without paying their hotel bills.

I was a spellbound listener during these daily sessions until Aunt Martha got on the subject of Mary Lee and her activities. I didn't want to hear about the plays she acted in, her dancing classes, her summer camp, her friends who took her to the Berkshires in the fall to enjoy the colors, and her skillful swimming. These were all things I longed to do but had no opportunity. I was wild with jealousy.

What could Mama brag about me? All I could do was cut stove wood the exact right length to fit the firebox of our cookstove and keep the woodbox filled. I knew how to feed cows, calves, pigs, and chickens. I could doctor hurt animals. I could clean the barn stalls and haul wheelbarrow loads of manure to the garden. I could pick cotton, hoe corn and velvet beans, and tote water from the big spring twice a day. I could crow so realistically that roosters from miles around answered me, and I talked to our dog Jack and the cats in their own language. But what was that compared to eating pastries in Pittsburgh tearooms, going to libraries full of books, and seeing talking pictures? Aunt Martha even had Mary Lee do some of her dances for us and recite some of her expression pieces. I hardened my vow to have nothing to do with her.

The upstairs bedroom was my refuge. Even though there was no door, the stairs turned so that Mary Alice and I had privacy. I went there to escape and be with my treasures: the hollow rocks I'd collected with beautiful colored sand in them, the petrified unicorn horn I'd found beyond the trestle under a cowcumber tree near the waterfall. On the windowsill above my bed I kept a collection of tiny glass bottles Mama saved for me from the kitchen. In them I mixed different ingredients, and after covering each bottle, I waited for the perfume I was sure they would produce. In a box under my bed my secret diary stayed hidden. On its pages I wrote my most private thoughts about our lives, my yearnings to become an actress on the stage, my longing for books, and my bitterness toward the Northerners who burned the University of Alabama's library in 1865. I had seen the mound on the university campus containing the ashes of six thousand books. I grieved because I had not a single book of my own. And Mary Lee was one of those Northerners. What I put in my diary was the real me, and I knew I'd be laughed at and ridiculed, or worse, pitied, so I guarded it. And also there was my drawing book Daddy had brought me, a big book that showed my progress as an artist. In the early days Mama showed me how to draw noses on my people and Daddy taught me to draw bird dogs. Now I drew scenes illustrating our daily lives like a diary in pictures.

Mary Lee had the run of our house and of our hill, but the one place she wasn't allowed was upstairs. She nagged to go up there. She tried to talk Mama into making me take her there. Mama said it was my business and let me be.

But one day as I lay on my bed drawing in my book, I heard a stairstep creak. Instantly I knew—Mary Lee. She was creeping up the stairs trying to catch me in my lair. In a flash I was off the bed and down the steps to meet her with a roar that made her turn and flee. After that I had to be constantly on guard. She was not going to give up. I was not going to give in. She learned which steps creaked and avoided them. Each time she tried, she came closer to reaching her goal. Then came the day she made it to the platform where the stairs turned left into our room without a door. She had never made it that far before so she didn't know a board creaked there too. I was on her quicker than a cat on a lizard. I said nothing. She said nothing. But we fell to. This time I was going to finish her off, once and for all. I was going to send her backwards down those twenty-one steps and break her neck, bust her backbone, snap her legs into little pieces like snapping green beans. I pushed with all my might to send her backwards. She pushed with all her might to come upwards. The only sound was the steady thunder of our bare feet on the hardwood floor.

In the kitchen Mama realized something was wrong. She came running down the hall, followed by Aunt Martha, and looked up. The fight had intensified because I knew it was now or never. Mama took the stairs three at a time and seized hold of me. She gave me a shake that brought me somewhat to my senses and propelled me up the few steps to the bedroom and shoved me on the bed where I lay panting. Aunt Martha dragged Mary Lee down the stairs, where to I didn't know or care.

Mary Lee never succeeded and we two cousins never made peace. Our mothers kept us carefully separated. When Mama had to go anywhere she took me with her and Mary Lee stayed with my sisters. At no time were we left together at home without a parent.

Though I never saw Mary Lee again after that summer, her dad stopped by our house on his way back to Pittsburgh from a Florida golfing holiday. He was dressed in golfing knickers with plaid knee socks and odd-looking shoes. We had seen pictures in the newspaper of people dressed that way. He and the friend with him stood by their big shiny car in the yard while we gathered round to talk. Suddenly Uncle Cliff pointed to me and said to his friend, "I want you to hear That One talk."

That One? Didn't he know my name? What was the matter with how I talked? I didn't say another word.

When Aunt Bessie, who was married to a Cox, heard about Mary Lee and me she laughed.

"They've both got Cox blood," she said, "so they come by that temper honest. I'm sure Martha understood. I've heard that when she gets mad she locks herself in the bedroom and bites pieces out of the dresser."

5

Ichabod Gets Lost

WHEN I WAS ABOUT TWELVE, Ichabod, my pet chicken, disappeared. As soon as I went into the backyard after school I knew he was missing. He always came to me, cheep-cheeping around my feet and scratching the ground with his little, crooked feet. Wherever I was working outside he was with me.

He should have been grown-up like his brother chickens but something went badly askew with his growth. His few feathers came out at all angles and most of him was naked. The other chickens bullied him and had pecked his head bloody before I found him. From that time on I guarded him. Each night I put him in a box, covered him with a soft rag, and set him behind the kitchen stove.

Near his bedtime, the evening star shone big and bright. I marveled at it, and at the fact that Roy in sixth grade, who helped his grandpa dig wells, claimed that from down in a well at brightest daylight you could see the stars shining. They were there all the time! I would think of this as I put Ichabod to bed singing his bedtime song softly, "Will there be any stars in my crown, in my crown, when at evening the sun goeth down . . ." I sang the song other times of day, too, peppy and loud, while I worked in the barn or the garden, or chopped wood in the backyard. And all the while little Ichabod scratched around my feet cheep, cheep, cheeping.

Immediately I notified everybody in the family that Ichabod was lost.

"It may be a fox caught him," Daddy said. "He can't see and didn't know the danger."

"He might have fallen in the old well," Mama suggested.

In our backyard was an abandoned well, dry as a desert. We dumped our trash in it. I hung my head over its crumbly edge, stared into its dark depths, and called him, but I couldn't see or hear anything.

"He wouldn't have run away," I whined. "He was too happy. I gave him everything he wanted."

So the days passed with me searching, waiting, and hoping. Distractions came. Strangers from far places wandered past on the highway, some going east, some going west. They needed food and water and often a place to spend the night. Those who were young and strong offered to work but others were too old or too sick.

One evening an elderly man with a long beard led a little girl, his granddaughter he explained later, up our lane and asked for food and lodging. Mama took them in, fixed them a supper, and gave them the best bed we had. We sat in front of the fire with them and talked a bit. The old man offered very little personal information. Mama never pried. After breakfast the next morning they trudged away with buttered biscuits filled with muscadine jelly in the grandpa's pocket for their lunch.

One early twilight I was splitting stove wood and thinking, "This is about the time Ichabod would be coming around for supper and to be put to bed." Unusual noises interrupted my thoughts. Hoofbeats! Around the corner of the house rode a woman in white on a big red horse. She dismounted slowly with a lot of saddle creaking, stretching her legs—I noticed her riding boots—and twisting her head and neck. I heard her give a deep sigh.

"I'm looking for Mr. and Mrs. Channel's place here in Brookwood," she said. "Can you direct me there?"

Mama, on her way to milk the cow, came out the kitchen door in time to hear her.

"Yes," Mama said. "You go past the fence corner, then past a field, and then the Channels are the second house on the left."

Mama gave the woman a cup of water, and while they talked, I stood beside her horse. I had to look up to study his big eyes, his soft nose, and his powerful neck, but he didn't invite me to touch him. I could see he was tired. Bundles were tied on the back of the saddle and a bag of hay hung against his side.

"It's been a long day," I heard the woman telling Mama. "I've come from over in Mississippi."

"Where are you going?" Mama asked.

"I'm riding from the West Coast to the East Coast," she said.

"That's a big job for you two to undertake."

"I realize that," the woman said. "But I stay with people along the way who put my horse up and feed me. Then they refer me to somebody ahead at the end of our day's ride. So far it's worked out fine." The woman smiled. "And it's almost finished."

As I lay in my warm bed that night I felt secure in the knowledge that the woman and Big Red were safe with the Channels. I hoped with all my heart that Ichabod, wherever he was, also slept safe after a tasty supper.

One morning two teenage boys stopped by asking for breakfast. They looked as though they'd slept in the woods. The boys said they were willing to work so Mama set them to digging postholes while she made a fire in the stove and cooked their food. Buddy was intrigued with the boys. He and my big orange cat watched them work, and the boys chatted with Buddy.

"When you were coming along the road did y'all see my sister's crooked chicken Ichabod anywhere?" I heard Buddy ask from where I sat on the porch shelling peas.

"We saw chickens, some of them run over," the towheaded boy said. "Did somebody steal Ichabod?"

"I think he run away," Buddy said. "Daddy thinks a fox got him. Mama thinks he's in the well. My sister cries over him."

"If we see him as we travel along, we'll send you word, okay?"

"What's your name?" the redheaded boy asked.

"My name's Buddy. His name's Thomas." I saw Buddy put his arm around my cat.

The redheaded boy paused in his digging and grinned at Buddy. "Thomas is my name too."

Buddy was thrilled. He jumped up and ran in the kitchen to tell Mama. "That redheaded boy is named for Thomas."

We were especially interested when two seamen from Mobile stopped in to ask for supper. We hoped they could tell us news of Daddy's brother Joe, but it turned out they didn't know him though they'd heard of his ship, the *Afoundria*. Because of their dirty selves (we could smell them), they refused to sit in chairs and instead hunched down on the kitchen floor and leaned against the wall while they ate. We offered them shelter for the night but they said they'd push on.

On days when Mary Alice and I hoed the corn and velvet beans in front of the house, we saw all kinds of men and boys hitchhiking on the road. Some of them wore suits and ties and carried a newspaper tucked under an arm and a briefcase in the non-thumbing hand. Others had on worn shirts and jeans or overalls and carried nothing. We'd look them over carefully, wondering where they were going and why.

"I wouldn't hire him," I'd say. "I wouldn't trust a worker with a mustache."

"Oh, I would," Mary Alice disputed. "He looks like a movie star."

Humans weren't the only creatures wandering. One day we found a small white goat in our field. Nobody we knew had goats. We ran him off twice, trying to make him go back home, wherever home was, but he stayed. He had a mind of his own. The chickens were goggle-eyed with amazement when he came into the yard. They crowded around the chicken house door cackling as if they were laughing, and in the yard they gathered around him in circles and carried on. The calves came to stare at him, and Jimmy-John, our calf that looked like a burro himself, chased him up on the wheelbarrow trying to find out what he was. My cat, Genevieve, who was in the house, hopped on the windowsill to stare and meow a question. The little creature butted around at will our collie and all the calves. Of course, we couldn't let him go hungry when everybody else was eating. So we fed him and gave him water and a safe place to sleep. He made himself right at home. After several weeks of us fattening him up, a man living on Covered Bridge Road came to claim him.

Some of the travelers traded their skills to the school for room and board in the community. One of them painted the school's plain brown stage curtain. He turned it into a beautiful scene with woods, a pond, and birds unknown to us. I watched him many days as I passed through the auditorium, fascinated to see him bring that picture out of nothing.

A theatrical group from up north brought trunks of costumes and stage settings with them and chose students for a play they would present for part of the profits. Local people gave them room and board while they directed the students, fitted them for costumes, rehearsed them, and set up the stage so pretty that we didn't recognize it. Jane was chosen for one of the leading parts.

Uncle Nathaniel and his wife Agnes happened to be visiting us from New York at that time. We all attended the play. Daddy was home which added to our pleasure. The play was presented only one night. The auditorium was crowded and hummed with excitement to see what these people from New York could do. We were not disappointed. It was wonderful. Agnes pronounced, "It was as good as any play I've seen on Broadway." She put into words what we all knew without ever seeing a Broadway play.

In between these visitations I did not forget my little Ichabod. I still searched for him wishing he'd come home somehow. I still sang his song as I went about my work hoping he'd hear and come. Finally I had to recognize that whatever happened to him, it wasn't possible for him to come back.

I was hiding in the barn crying when Daddy came to get the file to sharpen his hoe. He gave me comfort that I held on to for a long time.

"Sometimes we just have to give up," he said. "It looks as if he's gone for good. But you see those big thunderheads piled up in the sky? They look like whipped cream? Ichabod's probably resting on one of them waiting for you to fly by on your way to Heaven. When he sees you coming, he's going to hop out and put a star in your crown."

6

Home Remedies

ROZELLE GIVENS LIVED BELOW OUR hill on the way to the Quarters. He was small for his age and always playing alone in his yard. Sometimes I went to play with him. Before I left home, Mama made sure to remind me, "No matter how hot and thirsty you get, don't drink the Givenses' well water. There's something wrong with it." I could tell that was so just by looking at it—a dirty yellow color, thick as sorghum syrup, and slimy. I tasted it once. Ugh! How could they stand to drink it?

Rozelle didn't know many games, but he did love hide-and-go-seek so we played that often. He could run fast, and he laughed a lot, and I admired his even white teeth. I hoped he'd never take up snuff dipping. Both his parents dipped. They'd sit in their rocking chairs on their front porch, rocking and spitting a little, but swallowing a lot. I believed they swallowed so much snuff juice that it was turning them both the color of old hickory nut hulls. Sometimes they scrubbed their teeth with sweet gum toothbrushes but the brown stain remained on the few teeth they had left.

When I went to play with Rozelle, Mama would slip a treat in my overall pocket—small baked sweet potatoes or parched peanuts. After we finished playing, Rozelle and I would sit in the shade of the chinaberry tree for a picnic.

One day when Mama and I were searching the lower field for hen nests, we came up to the barbwire fence that separated our field from the Givenses' yard. Mrs. Givens was bent double over the rubboard, washing clothes. We didn't want to interfere with her work, but we did ask about Rozelle as we didn't see him about anywhere.

"He's kinda puny today," his mother said. "So he's staying in bed."

"Too bad," Mama said. "What seems to be his trouble?"

"Just a sore throat. And he feels hot like he might have a little fever," Mrs. Givens said. "I think he's going to be all right terrectly."

But several days later when we were hoeing our corn patch we knew Rozelle wasn't all right because parked at the Givenses' gate was Dr. Pruitt's old car, a tall, enclosed two-passenger Model T Ford. He would drive it along the road at about fifteen miles an hour with his assistant, Mrs. Dawson, sitting straight as a poker beside him. Some people called Dr. Pruitt a quack, but in desperate cases they sent for him. What did this mean for Rozelle? Two days later Daddy heard at the store that little Rozelle was dead. Diphtheria, people said.

"They didn't take him to the schoolhouse on inoculation day," Mama said, shaking her head sadly.

I well remembered that summer day when the Tuscaloosa County Health Department nurses came to the schoolhouse and gave the shots. There was lots of boo-hooing, and temper fits as well, so some parents didn't make their children take the shots. Other parents were afraid the vaccinations might stunt their children's growth or turn them into dummies.

That needle going in my arm did sting, but the alcohol felt cool, and I was fascinated to think that the invisible, tiny mites in that serum would spread through my body and keep the sickness away.

It wasn't only the children of poor folks like Rozelle who died from not getting vaccinated. The storekeeper's daughter, Bobbie Ophelia, who was as pretty as her name, died in 1932. I had often seen her in the afternoon, dressed in ruffles and lace, playing among the flowers in her yard. My sister Francys joined the neighbors to sit up all night with Bobbie Ophelia in her flower-lined coffin before her burial. "She looked just as natural as she did in life, surrounded by flowers," Francys told me.

But there were other dangers round about us besides diphtheria. My classmate, Johnny, got a splinter stuck in his foot. All of us got splinters and we did what Johnny's sister did. She took a needle and dug out the splinter. But Johnny's foot didn't get well. Red streaks went up his leg. Soon Johnny couldn't walk very well, and he died of lockjaw, a sickness as feared as a mad-dog bite.

Another classmate, Clarence, took a hurting in his right side. The pains were so bad he was bent double. After many days of suffering Clarence died of appendicitis.

Then one day, Nina, an older girl in Francys's class, missed school on account of sickness. She lay in bed so listless and quiet that everybody thought it was the heat. "She'll feel better when fall comes," her mother said. Mama and Francys went to see Nina, taking a bouquet of flowers from our yard. Nina smiled at them but said nothing.

Then we heard that Nina had died. Her mother told us about her death at church.

"After I got the other young'uns off on their way to school I was cleaning up in the kitchen. Nina called me to her bed, so soft I barely heard her. 'Mama,' she whispered, 'Listen to that beautiful music.' I listened but couldn't hear a thing. She shook my arm. 'Listen, listen. I never heard such a sweet sound. It's telling me to come, Mama.' And while I held her hand she just died, breaking my heart that she was so willing to go."

"But she's in Heaven now where all is joy," the preacher comforted her. "Think of the suffering she's missed in this vale of tears."

And we joined him in praying Nina on her way. I imagined her surrounded by angels making music as they escorted her to Heaven, leaving her mama behind.

Everybody knew how much we country people needed a doctor, but there was not one for us. Each family had to develop their own remedies. At our house Mama's turpentine bottle was always available. We used the piney-smelling turpentine for boils, cat scratches and bites, and stumped toes. We even rubbed it on our chests when we had a rattling cough. Other families too depended on their turpentine bottles. In winter, with the windows closed tight, our classroom smelled like a turpentine still.

Also in our medicine chest was a small bottle so old I could barely make out the label: "Paregoric." We knew it was a bad dope of some kind, but when we children tossed and turned at night because of a toothache, Daddy would soak a tuft of cotton in paregoric and stuff it in our decayed tooth. Before long we'd slip off into a comforting sleep.

One or the other of us usually had a sore throat which we soothed by gargling with warm salt water. If that didn't cure us, Daddy made a brush of twisted cotton on the end of a sweet gum stem and swabbed our throats with iodine. I knew that iodine was poison but I knew too that my daddy was careful, and almost always we recovered quickly after his treatment.

Besides salt, we took baking soda out of the kitchen cupboard for heartburn, for bad breath, and for brushing our teeth. When we were sick enough to stay home from school, Mama cooked us chicken soup and sometimes boiled custard that tasted like melted vanilla ice cream only better. Mama's food made being sick worthwhile.

Not all the children I knew were so blessed. I was glad I didn't live with Ruby and Walter, my sometimes playmates across the road. Their mother kept a store of home remedies ready for any of their ailments and her children were expected to help replenish her supply. The one plant she didn't want them touching was jimson weed. It grew nearly everywhere. To me it wasn't a weed but a beautiful flower. However, we were taught from our beginning that every part of it was poisonous. I often looked longingly at its large white trumpet flowers wondering how they smelled but dared not smell even one. Ruby's mother pulled up the plants and hung them on the back porch to dry. Then when one of her terrible asthma attacks was coming on, she burned the dried leaves in a bucket, smothering them so that they made a dense smoke in her closed bedroom. Ruby and Walter had to help her keep the smoke going and sometimes they beat her on the back with flat cans of sardines to help her breathe. Often during such an attack they ran to our house to ask Mama to come help them. Mama never talked about these sessions. What I learned came from the little that Ruby and Walter said. Hearing their comments was like hearing a nightmare someone had. They kept a supply of hand-rolled jimson weed cigarettes ready in case their mother was seized by an asthma attack when they were in school.

Usually when we went out to play in the community and the woods, Ruby and Walter had to bring a paper poke for collecting. The most important thing we were to watch for was white dog droppings. They were uncommon. I never learned what kind of dog left behind white "dookie," as Walter called it. With the least sign of sickness, their mother brewed white dog tea from it for them to drink.

One day I asked Ruby, "What does white dog tea taste like?" She didn't answer—just screwed up her face in an ugly way and stuck out her tongue.

Their mother's remedy for earache was about as bad as white dog tea. She told the one who was sick to find a betsy bug. She then twisted off its head, turned it upside down, and squeezed three drops of bug blood into the hurting ear.

I was amazed. "I didn't know bugs had blood," I said to Ruby.

"Well, something comes out," she said. "Ma calls it blood."

Another danger that beset all country people was snake bite. The most accepted snake bite medication was alcohol. Though Alabama was a dry state, many men of the community carried a bottle of wild-cat whiskey in their pockets in case of need.

The state law did allow each householder to make a few gallons of wine each year, usually from muscadines, which we gathered free from the wild. The problem with our family was we enjoyed the muscadines themselves so much we never got home from the woods with enough to make wine.

Galls from oak trees were another thing we looked for in the fall. Oak gall tea was a remedy for rheumatism. It was so bitter that I was sure galls were the source of the saying "Bitter as gall." But oldsters afflicted with crippling pain didn't hesitate to drink it.

Warts were so common among us that almost every family had several solutions for them. Our family believed that playing with toad frogs could be responsible. Because Mary Alice played with them and had warts, I didn't play with them, and I didn't have warts. Trying to help Mary Alice, we sisters pricked each of her warts, put a drop of its blood on an individual pebble, tied all the pebbles in a rag and dropped the bundle on a well-traveled path. The warts were then transmitted to the person who found the bundle and opened it out of curiosity. That didn't seem fair, but when you had a passel of warts to get rid of you didn't think about fairness.

The only horrors of summer that we had no home remedy for were the bites of "mad dogs," which carried rabies, and black widow spiders.

Those of us who survived childhood rejoiced to see doctors become more accessible to country people. But we did admit that some of the medicines prescribed by modern doctors tasted as putrid as white dog tea must have and cost money to boot!

7

Summer of Decision

WALKING HOME FROM SCHOOL ONE afternoon in May 1933 my feet felt as heavy as the load I was carrying. It was the last day of school. I had cleaned my desk of the year's accumulation of papers, books, artwork, and everything else, and was bringing it home. It was not a day of celebration for me. I dreaded many things about summer: The long, empty weeks of field work in the heat, the explosive lightning storms, and the protracted revival meetings that were the most dreaded of the Dreads. Already the tent was going up in the forks of the road near Virgie's grandparents' house. I paused to watch for a moment the men working to get it in place, remembering how it would be.

But this summer was different. I had reached twelve, the age of accountability. I had to make a decision.

As soon as the tent was established the meetings began. A Methodist minister and a Baptist minister were in charge. They gave a picnic at the big spring "for all children under ninety" and most of our family attended. I knew I'd feel better if I went too, seeing people I knew and eating hot dogs and toasting marshmallows, but I was postponing the meeting as long as I could. My sisters came home all pepped up after a good time and ready for the two weeks ahead.

Things went well for the first week. The weather stayed calm, crowds overflowed the tent, heathen boys hung around outside commenting on what went on during the service, laughing and smoking their cigarettes. Inside, the faithful ones gave testimonies as to what their Christian life meant to them, some who had family feuds begged forgiveness and were reconciled, and tears were shed. One night huge bouquets of ferns and flowers decorated the platform where the ministers stood. They explained that this was "Appreciation Night" when everyone should take flowers from the bouquets to pin on those persons who had done the most for them. The organist played softly while the congregation fell apart, laughing, shouting, and crying.

The second week the preachers got down to business. They preached more earnestly, pleaded more eloquently, and threatened with power, working up to that last night. And on that last night I was late for the service. I had hung back as long as I could but I knew I had to go. The tent was crowded but Mary Alice had saved me a place beside her. I could feel a tense expectancy like an electric current in the air. The Methodist minister was holding forth but he was young and lacking in fire. When the wizened Baptist preacher took over the platform things heated up. He seemed to speak to each one of us painting a word picture of what awaited the unsaved in Hell. Even the children fell silent and no babies whimpered.

By this time the preacher was stomping back and forth across the platform hollering at times and slamming the Bible on the pulpit as he passed it. But it was worse when he leaned out toward us and whispered, hissing like the serpent in Eden. At one of these times I heard the thunder. A storm! It came up fast. The closer it got, the brighter and more intense the lightning. To my terrified eyes it seemed to aim for the tent pole. The powerful wind thrashed the tent flaps.

The tent itself billowed and rolled, threatening to collapse on everybody. Doomsday was here, now! Weaving in and out of the turmoil were the shouts of the saved and the speaking in tongues of the specially gifted. A woman, worn thin by hard work and burned brown by the sun, thrashed around on the ground, bleating in ecstasy.

Now the preacher had to shout louder to be heard. "What if you don't make it home tonight? Lightning could strike you right where you sit. And who knows what dangers are waiting for you out there in the dark?" He wiped the sweat from his face. "You're never forewarned when you'll take your last breath. And oh, how sad if you go unbaptized and unrepentant." He softened his voice, pleading. "I want to meet you up there. I want to sit down with you by the River of Life and smile as I shake your hand and say, 'Remember that night in Brookwood? That night you claimed the Lord?'" He paused, looking out over the crowd with tear-filled eyes. "But what if I don't find you there? Think of me with a broken heart sitting alone by that Great River, waiting, watching . . ." He wiped his face again with his big white handkerchief.

The Methodist minister took over, announcing the invitation hymn. Its words warning us to "turn not away to Life's sparkling cup" stuck in my craw because it was Life's sparkling cup I longed for. To be good was the dominant plea of my prayers, yet I had learned early the belief that the good die young and I wanted to live. My soul was grievously torn.

But I knew I had no choice. I had to make my move. Mary Alice, standing beside me, looked frozen in place.

"I'm going," I said through stiff lips and stepped out in the aisle. She followed me down that endless way to the cadence of the woeful words wailed by the congregation, "Oh, how sad to face the judgment, unprepared to meet thy God . . ."

I grasped the outreaching hand of the Baptist minister while Mary Alice shook the hand of the Methodist preacher.

"Which church?" one of them said.

"Big Hurricane Baptist," I gasped, as a bolt of lightning reached in for us.

"Turn around now," he said. We faced the audience of curious and pious. The minister spoke but thunder shook the tent and drowned out his announcement. He started over. "Aileen and Mary Alice Kilgore present themselves for baptism."

I knew that a testimony was customary now but my brain was paralyzed. What could I say? I hadn't had any revelation like Paul, no loving voice spoke and took away my temper, hatefulness, and greed, and made me good. I just knew I didn't want to go to Hell. The storm was on top of us now as we stood there clinging to each other. Maybe that was why the preacher didn't ask for our testimony but called for the closing hymn and everybody hurried out in the night to walk home.

The ordeal wasn't over yet. The date was set for our baptism in Big Hurricane Creek and Mama got us ready. She bought many yards of a thin material called unbleached domestic from Brown's Basement at ten cents a yard to make our robes. She gathered them at the shoulders so that the soft cloth fell to our feet covering us completely. Inside the hems she sewed heavy lead sinkers like the ones we used when we played pitching washers. Their weight would keep our gowns from floating up in the water and revealing our underwear to the people watching on both banks of the creek.

Doubts and fears haunted us as we watched the robes take shape. At night Mary Alice and I whispered to one another in bed: We didn't know how to swim. What if the preacher dropped us and we drowned? What if a cottonmouth moccasin came after us? The creek was full of them and they resented humans invading their territory. What if one of those quick lightning storms came up while we were in the water? Water attracted lightning, we knew. It was no comfort to remember Mama's admonition: "If lightning strikes you, you'll never know it."

All of our worry was wasted. Baptism day came anyway.

That Sunday afternoon, we arrived on time at the Wildsmith house where we changed into our robes in a back room with Mama overseeing us. We walked down to the creek barefoot. Allie's daddy, Deacon Amos, was there to help us into the creek and lead us to where Preacher Riley was waiting out in the middle of the stream.

On the way I whispered, "Did you run all the snakes away?"

"Don't you know the Lord would lock their mouths tight shut to protect you?" Deacon Amos reproved me.

"I'm not sure He knows I'm here among them," I said.

"Of course He knows. In His word He says He will give His angels charge over you to keep you in all your ways. Don't you remember?"

"Now I do," I said taking heart.

"And nobody's drowned yet," he added.

There's always the first time, said the Ole Imp who lurked in my head, but I refused to listen.

Brother Riley prayed, committing us to the same watery grave with our Savior. He reminded us that when John the Baptist baptized Him the sky opened up and a Voice spoke. I hadn't thought of that. We were following in the footsteps of Jesus!

Neither of us choked or drowned or got snakebit. And our gowns didn't flare up and reveal us to the onlookers.

Back at the house we dried off and redressed. In the blurred mirror of the Wildsmith's bedroom I saw no difference in my looks—no shining radiance, no halo, just the same old freckled face that Great-uncle Pat had pronounced the ugliest he'd ever seen. When was my transformation going to take place?

I would just have to wait and see.

8

Thanksgiving Day

ON OUR FARM IN TUSCALOOSA County we had sixteen acres of land ready for plowing. The problem was we had no way to plow. Among the cobwebs of our barn stood a plow stock and an assortment of plows. On a nearby nail hung a halter and a harness but the mule stall was empty. And a mule we had to have to pull the plow so we could plant the crops we depended on to feed our family of seven and our cows, pigs, and chickens. But mules cost money and as the Great Depression dragged on we had no money.

Help came from an unexpected source: our dead grandfather. I knew little about him. He drank whiskey, gambled on the Tombigbee River steamboats, and every pig-killing season gave chitling feasts that were famous in Pickens County. After his death he unintentionally gifted our family with a small black mule named Li'l Gal. He had bought her for White Owl Mine at Klondike, Alabama, but the mine owners never paid him. Daddy reclaimed her and led her two miles home along the Birmingham Highway.

But Li'l Gal's work in the mine didn't fit her to be a plow mule. She had trained herself to be watchful and fast to avoid being crushed by the mining cars. In the field she went at a run and wore Daddy out. Uncle Davis, over in Walker County, ordered a Sears and Roebuck wagon and had it sent to us. It arrived disassembled with a set of instructions.

"Maybe our mule'll be better at pulling a wagon than she is at plowing," Daddy said as we children watched him fit the wagon pieces together and oil the wheels. The completed red-and-cream wagon looked splendid. We couldn't wait to try it out. Our chance came Thanksgiving Day 1933.

That day Virgie, my classmate, came to our house. Daddy suggested we take the wagon to the far woods for a load of pine straw to spread in our cow stalls and for rich pine knots to burn in the cookstove. We children dropped everything we were doing to collect rakes, shovels, and tow sacks. Daddy hitched Li'l Gal to the wagon. We tied our collie, Jack, to the chinaberry tree to keep him at home to protect Mama and our baby brother.

Then we climbed aboard. Daddy said, "Giddyup," and off we rolled. Li'l Gal pulled us across several fields, the wheels turning silently and moving us right along into a woods at Howton where we raked the clean-smelling straw, stuffed it into tow sacks, and searched the underbrush for the rich pine knots. We did a lot of shouting, laughing, and playing. We fought a pine cone war, Francys and Jane versus Mary Alice, Virgie, and me. We were winning when I noticed a bunch of boys under a distant grove of huge old trees that looked half-dead.

"What're they doing?" I asked.

"I can't tell," said Jane, squinting her eyes to see better. "They're picking up things."

"I see Archie. He's in my class," Francys said, looking hard at the distant boys. "Let's go find out."

We straggled over, full of curiosity. The boys stopped what they were doing as we got closer, and scruffy Willett from my class snarled, "This is Howton—no Brookwooders allowed." I made a cross-eyed face at him and turned my back.

"We're getting chestnuts," Archie said, tilting his five-gallon bucket to show us a bunch of prickly brown things almost as big as baseballs. "Look at these stickers." He picked up one of the balls with his gloved hand. "You have to be careful 'cause they sure can hurt." He showed us another burr that had burst open revealing a plump, shiny brown nut. "But, boy hidy, are they good eating."

The other boys who gathered around us were each wearing one glove too, ragged but thick.

"Some people call them porcupine eggs," one of the boys said.

"Why're the trees dying?" I asked.

"The blight, dummy," Willett said. "Don't you know nothin'?"

I snarled, pulling back my lips to show my tushes. "Go jump in the Black Warrior River," I said.

"A blight's killing American chestnuts everywhere," Archie said. "In a couple of years all these will be just two rows of giant skeletons."

"Indians musta planted them," a tall boy with spectacles said. "Long time ago. They used to live where my house is. We find arrowheads all the time."

"Yeah, and pieces of pottery, and spearheads," added another boy.

"How about war clubs?" I asked.

"Not yet," said Archie, "but we keep looking."

My arms reached only partway round one of the giants that was losing its bark. "What a beauty you musta been," I said sadly, laying my cheek against its trunk.

"They *were* beautiful." Archie turned to Francys. "Remember that poem we had to learn, 'Under the spreading chestnut tree, the village smithy stands'?"

Francys nodded.

"Daddy's calling us," Jane said. "He's ready to go."

Willett and I exchanged another ugly face, my sisters gave little goodbye waves, and we ran back to our wagon.

I thought Li'l Gal strained to pull our load home so I got off the wagon to walk with Daddy.

"Our wagon doesn't weigh near what a loaded coal car weighs," he comforted me, "so Li'l Gal isn't hurting."

A one-eyed old man with a skin-and-bones mule waited for us in our yard.

"Pierson's my name," he said to Daddy. "Since you ain't a reg'lar farmer I declared I'd see about trading a horse I got in my barn lot at home for this work mule o' yours."

"Don't know what use I'd have for a horse," Daddy said, "but have a seat on the steps and we'll see. You young'uns unload while I let Li'l Gal drink and roll in the dust."

I patted Mr. Pierson's weary-looking mule.

"What's her name?" I asked.

"Ada. She's real gentle. Wanna ride?"

"Sure 'nuff," I said.

Mr. Pierson helped Virgie and me onto Ada's bony back and we rode down in our field. Broom sedge grew everywhere, a bright russet that waved in the wind. I was instantly transformed into a Wild West cowboy on a spirited Spanish mustang. I kicked poor old Ada in the side to put some mustang spirit into her and off we went, riders of the purple sage, in our imagination leaving our farm behind.

Too soon Jane brought us back to reality by yelling from the yard, "He wants his mule." Reluctantly we rode Ada back.

"Did they trade?" I asked Jane. She shook her head no and went back in the house.

Mr. Pierson reached for Ada's rope. I wouldn't let go. "How 'bout letting us ride Ada home for you?"

"Awright," he said, and we set out along the highway with him walking beside us.

As we passed Virgie's grandmother's house, the Smith place, we noticed lots of cars parked in the yard. Virgie said, "It must be near dinnertime. We'd better get off here."

I grinned my thanks to Mr. Pierson as I handed him the rope and we jumped off. Ada gave a deep sigh.

"She's glad to be rid of us," Virgie said.

We slipped inside the dining room to take two chairs near the end of the table. Liza, the teenage Black girl in the kitchen who was sometimes our playmate, was carrying a big bowl of chicken and dressing which she plopped down on the already loaded table.

"Wash your hands," she ordered knowing us too well.

Returning with hands clean of Ada odor, pine knot dust, pine cone resin, and all the other stuff we'd handled that morning, we sat down for the blessing then applied ourselves to the food.

The dining room was large and the table was long but it still felt crowded because the Smith boys were all so big, not fat, but tall and wide. Mr. Smith, most imposing of all due to his Native American ancestors, filled his chair at the head of the table. Down the line toward

Virgie and me were Murray, Oscar, Joe, John, and various men relatives I didn't know, some with wives and children who were too young to interest us.

Virgie's daddy wasn't there. Years ago he went away to hunt for work and never came back. I didn't miss him but sometimes Virgie went off into the woods to cry.

Adult conversation swirled all around mixed with the clacking of forks on plates and ice tinkling in tea glasses. Virgie's mother and Liza moved around the table filling everybody's need for more while Mrs. Smith sat at the foot of the table, her sharp eyes missing nothing. She was short and puffy: white hair puffed about her pink face and ended in a neat ball atop her head, sleeves puffed over arms that were never still, and a pleated apron puffed over her hips and down to the hem of her long dress. Except for fragmentary whispers about our plans for the afternoon—games! play!—Virgie and I concentrated on eating.

As soon as we finished the sweet potato pie, we slipped away from the table and ran outside to meet Virgie's cousins. We spent the afternoon wearing ourselves out playing hide-and-seek, my favorite as I was clever at finding hiding places behind the trees in the orchard, inside the corncrib, the smokehouse, the toolshed, and, one time, the privy. I was the fastest runner and always won the race "home" after being discovered. We played hopscotch awhile then shot some marbles. I kept my marbles in a Bull Durham tobacco bag with a drawstring top. I loved the speejinks, small clay marbles as plain as I was. But my taw, the main marble I shot with, was large, beautiful, and made of glass. We didn't play for keeps—that was forbidden—but just for fun. We knew our marbles so well that we never got them mixed up with anybody else's.

About midafternoon we went in the kitchen for a drink of water and maybe a leftover piece of pie and found Liza hanging up the dishrag and putting away the dishpan. We tagged her and she chased us into the yard popping us with the dishtowel, making us squeal every time she stung us. She had good aim.

The grown-ups were all either talking lazily on the wide front porch or napping in a quiet corner, and paid us no mind. Finally in the shade of a catalpa tree we collapsed laughing and breathless to listen to the fishing worms munching on the leaves overhead.

After a while Liza stretched her long skinny body and sat up. "I got to get on home. Got to make tracks before dark."

She went in the kitchen to get the leftovers for her own family's Thanksgiving dinner and started on her two-mile walk. We didn't want to give her up and walked along the road beside her till I looked back and saw Mary Alice coming into the Smith yard carrying our empty water buckets and followed by Jack waving his plumy tail.

"Mama said for us to get to the spring before dark," she hollered. "And come right home."

I looked around. It *was* getting late. I feared for night to catch us in the woods. I hurried back for my bucket. We called Jack and trudged downhill through the still trees to the spring.

That night when I crawled into bed, adjusting the long bolster down the middle to keep Mary Alice from kicking me in her dreams, I laid my head on the pillow, closed my eyes, and thought in capital letters, "SO ENDS A HAPPY THANKSGIVING DAY!"

9

Mary Alice Goes into Business

WE WERE STILL AT THE breakfast table when Teensy rode into our yard on her scruffy bull calf, Buck, leading another bull calf that looked like Buck's twin. Mary Alice ran out to meet her and I followed.

Teensy grinned so wide I thought the freckles would pop off her face. "This here is Buddy," she said. "I been training him for you to ride. And now he's graduated. Let's go pick up bottles."

Mary Alice took Buddy's rope and looked him over. Teensy dismounted and tied Buck to the chinaberry tree.

"Come have some breakfast," Mama said.

While Teensy ate a buttered biscuit with muscadine jelly, Mary Alice changed into a clean shirt and got a feed sack out of the barn to put bottles in.

"What you going to do with bottles?" I asked.

"We gonna sell them to Aleck," Teensy said, reaching for another biscuit. Mama buttered it for her and spread it with the dark-red jelly.

"I forgot to tell you," Mary Alice said to me. "Aleck'll buy any bottles we find and he'll pay good. But they have to be clean, and he'll pay more if they have a lid."

Francys was clearing the table to wash the dishes. She looked at Mama who was getting ready to churn the clabbered sweet milk into butter and buttermilk. "You think that's safe, Mama? He's a whiskey maker."

That wasn't all. Everybody knew that years ago he'd gone to Texas to make his fortune. Instead, he got put in the penitentiary. When Ma

Ferguson became governor of Texas, she offered to pardon Aleck if he agreed to leave Texas and never come back. That suited him just fine. Next thing anybody in Brookwood knew he was home wearing decorated cowboy boots and a cowboy hat, setting up his still just over the hill from our house and going into business.

Mama shrugged at Francys's question. "There're worse things in these hard times. You girls be careful. Aleck will see to it that his customers behave."

As the girls rode bareback and shoeless down the lane in their ragged sun hats and bib overalls, Jane and I watched them. Mary Alice had stumped her big toe the day before and had a clean rag tied around it so that she appeared to have a white bunny rabbit riding on her foot. We smothered our laughter not wanting to hurt their feelings.

"I wish we could make their picture," I said.

Their first trip set the pattern for all the collecting trips that followed. Teensy and Buck rode on one side of the highway and Mary Alice and Buddy took the other, each keeping a sharp lookout for the glitter of glass along the shoulder of the road as well as off in the grass and bushes.

Snakes were on their minds too as some of the search places were marshy. By dinnertime they usually had covered their territory and taken their haul to the big spring for washing. They set their morning's collection out in the sun of our backyard while they ate dinner. In the afternoon they rode over the hill to Aleck's place to make their delivery and collect their pay.

I had seen Aleck's place, an unpainted shotgun house mounted on rock pillars, from a distance when I'd been searching for our guinea nests. I didn't go close for fear he'd think I was spying out his still and that would have been dangerous. Stills had to be kept secret because they were illegal.

The girls had no fears. After their transaction with Aleck, they relaxed on the edge of his porch, swinging their legs and observing what went on around them. No matter what time of day they were there, customers sat around on the porch drinking and talking, or some were passed out lying on the floor. What the girls wanted was to see Aleck's still, but no matter how they begged, they could never persuade him to take them to it. Those of us at home were glad he didn't. The less they knew about his business, the better.

Every day that they went bottling they could find some jars and bottles, but their most profitable time was during football season, especially when the game was in Birmingham or Tuscaloosa. The narrow, twisting highway made traffic through Brookwood bumper-to-bumper and very slow, so the car occupants had plenty of time to drink and discard their bottles. And the bottles they discarded were prize specimens because they were store-bought whiskey bottles. Aleck paid well for those discards.

While they were still in the bottle business, Daddy brought another business opportunity their way. When the railroad didn't need him he worked on a WPA project at the university. Several of his coworkers paid thirty cents a day to ride to work with him. During the chilly winter days they spoke longingly of sassafras tea, remembering it as a tonic from their childhood. Daddy, knowing how Mary Alice and Teensy ranged the countryside on their mounts, asked them if they wanted to dig some sassafras roots for his passengers.

The girls set right to work. They took a pick and rode to the big ditch above the spring where sassafras grew in abundance. Very little digging was needed to harvest the roots out of the red clay as erosion had exposed many of them. When they had a bagful of roots, they washed them at the spring and brought them to our house to dry on newspapers in the shade. Mama helped them tie the clean roots in bundles with string she had unraveled from feed sacks, and price each bundle. Then Daddy delivered them.

The girls dug roots until the sap rose and the plants needed it to make leaves and blossoms and berries. They had no trouble dividing the profits equally from their bottle business and their root business even though Teensy didn't go to school and Mary Alice wasn't good at arithmetic. Mr. Martz welcomed their business at his store and we welcomed what they shared with us at home. Mary Alice bought one of his tablets with a pretty cover of a house on blue Lake Capri and a soft lead pencil for keeping a record of their income and what they bought: hoop cheese, crackers, Dr. Peppers, and all kinds of candies, Moon Pies, and cookies. Mary Alice especially enjoyed drinking the Nehi Orange "dope," as we called soda. "It's not really knee-high," she confided to us at supper. "But it's plenty big." Their money didn't stay in their overall pockets very long but all of us enjoyed it while they had it.

10

Miss Know-It-All

I KNEW I WASN'T POPULAR. Everybody preferred my pretty sisters and I thought it was because I wasn't pretty. Great-uncle Pat, who visited us from the Delta, impressed me with that fact when I was seven. Passing by his chair where he sat with his ear trumpet, I was so absorbed in playing that I didn't notice him. He reached out his walking stick, caught me around the neck with the crook, and pulled me to him. For several minutes he stared into my face before pushing me away.

"Ugliest child I ever saw in my life," he announced.

That didn't mean much to me then. I went on playing, but as time passed I noticed how often I was left out and overlooked. I thought my ugliness must be the reason. The real reason never occurred to me till one day when Mama got exasperated with me. She called me Miss Know-It-All. Coming from Mama I knew it had to be the truth.

I didn't mean to be a know-it-all. I just wondered about things out loud. For example, New Year's Day. We always had hog jowl, black-eyed peas, and collards. We stuffed ourselves on the peas for the silver money they would bring us in the new year and ate a good supply of collards to make more greenbacks with our name on them. The years of the Depression passed slowly by, New Year's Day after New Year's Day, and we seemed to get poorer and poorer. No matter how we overstuffed ourselves with all that food, it made no difference whatever. But I was the only one who pointed that out.

Then there were dreams. If we had a good dream, we always told it loud and detailed before breakfast so it would come true. Bad dreams, if told at all, had to wait till after breakfast. None of our good dreams ever came true but we kept on with the custom, and nobody but me said anything.

And there was Daddy's coffee. Every morning that he was home, when one of us filled his coffee cup he watched for the money to appear. Sometimes it was a small circle of cream-colored bubbles the size of a nickel that rose to the top of his coffee, but at other times the cluster of bubbles was big as a half-dollar.

"Gee whiz," Daddy would marvel. "Look at all that money coming my way today." But at the end of day when we gathered at the supper table for cornbread and buttermilk, no money had come to his hand.

One morning when I took the coffee pot back to the kitchen to set it on the stove, I said to Mama, "What a waste of words! All he gets is that same four and a half dollars a week on WPA. Five days' work. Not even a dollar a day! Why does he keep saying that?"

"Hush up!" Mama hissed. "If thinking that helps your daddy get through his workday, you just be quiet, Miss Know-It-All."

I couldn't understand people fooling themselves. For a long time I had believed and hoped in the buzzard rhyme: "One for sorrow, two for joy, three for a letter, four for a boy, five for silver, six for gold, seven for a secret that's never been told." But finally I accepted that the number of buzzards I could count in the sky had nothing to do with what happened to me.

Even so, at first I paid no attention to Mama calling me that name. Then one winter morning at school when we were assembling for class Barney announced, "Ever' night there's a cross on the moon. I've seen it. Grandpa says that means the world's coming to an end, and soon too." I stared at him in disbelief. "You look tonight," he said. "You'll see it. If there's a circle around the moon, however many stars in that circle says how many days before it happens."

At supper that night after Daddy said the blessing, as we crumbled cornbread into our buttermilk, I shared what Barney had said.

"It's a clear sky tonight," I said. "The moon ought to be rising soon. I'm sure gonna see that cross."

I looked out of every window in the living room, and sure enough, from every one of them I could see a bright cross shining from the full moon as plain as the nose on my face. I didn't believe it. For one thing, I wasn't ready for the world to end. I wouldn't accept its ending without a struggle. I went into the unheated bedrooms and looked from the windows in there. Yep, the cross was still there. Back in the warm living room while looking out the cold windowpane again, the thought came to me: *Go outside and look.* I started for the front door.

"Don't go out without a wrap," Great-aunt Mittie, visiting us from Pickens County, warned.

"I'll just be a minute," I said bracing myself against the icy air. As soon as I was in the open on the grassy yard I looked up. I wanted to crow with joy—no cross! The windowpane glass must have done something to put that cross on the moon. I went back inside to the bedroom and looked. The cross had reappeared. I raised the window. Sure enough, it disappeared.

At school the next day nearly everybody had looked out their home windows and seen the cross. Each one was trying to tell about it and what their papa or grandpa thought about it. When I could get a word in edgewise about my discovery the class stared at me speechless. "You're lying," Barney finally said, looking at me sourly.

No matter how I insisted, nobody believed me. Even the next day after some of them had seen for themselves that I was right, they didn't want to talk about it. Then the full moon passed, the nights clouded up, and we had snow.

In the excitement of the snowfall the cross was forgotten, but I wasn't forgiven. To myself I vowed to hold my tongue.

That vow flew out of my mind when Florrie Ann told the class about a big elm tree near Birmingham that had a sword in it.

"A man was going away to the war," she said, "and he told his sweetie and ever'body else 'I'm goin' to leave it there till I get back, after I whip those blue belly Yankees.' The tree grew and grew around it, getting bigger and bigger, but he didn't ever come home from the war and it's still there."

Right then and there I was determined to see that piece of history even though I wondered why a man going away to fight would leave his sword behind. Wouldn't he need it in battle? When some other students wanted to see the sword too, Florrie Ann agreed to ask her uncle, whose workplace was near the tree, to take us. Uncle Dennis loved history and was proud to be our guide.

The day was set and we gathered at a school bus stop to wait for him. When he pulled off onto the shoulder of the road in his pickup he didn't get out. "Climb in the back and scrooch down," he hollered. "And don't be jumping around, y'hear?"

The sun was hot but the wind was cooling. We were too busy looking at the unfamiliar scenery to do any jumping around. We waved at the few cars that passed us and laughed when somebody waved back. In my mind was the thought of that sword: Would it have jewels in the handle like Excalibur, King Arthur's sword? Would we be able to touch it? How I wished we had a Kodak to make its picture!

Uncle Dennis parked near some ramshackledy houses. Nobody was in sight. We jumped out, straightened our legs, and followed him to a big tree. We stood around it in respectful silence looking up.

"There it is," Uncle Dennis said proudly. "See it sticking out of the trunk?" And he retold the story of the noble soldier-to-be who put it there and vowed to leave it till he came back victorious.

I strained my eyes. During the years since it was put there the wood and bark of the elm had grown around most of it leaving the handle and part of the blade showing. What I saw was a crushing disappointment. No jeweled handle but that wasn't all.

"That's no sword," I snarled, throwing my sweaty sun hat on the ground. "That's a—a—scythe, what you hold in your hand to cut weeds. I use one every day to cut grass for our cows." In my rage I couldn't stop blabbing. "Besides that, if a fellow's going away to fight, he needs his sword. Why would he stick it in a tree and leave it behind?"

Emma began to cry. "It's such a pretty story," she sniffled. "Why'd you have to spoil it?"

Everybody was deflated, especially Florrie Ann. And I thought for a minute Uncle Dennis wasn't going to let me climb back in the pickup. We dragged home in the heat without saying much.

Later when I asked Aunt Mittie why nobody wanted to know the truth, she said, "Sometimes life's so hard people need a 'pretty story' to help them hold on to a little hope." After a short silence she said,

"Do you like the stories I tell you chirren before bedtime?"

"Oh, yes!" I said.

"What are they usually about?" she asked.

"Ohhh, castles and kings and queens, rooms full of gold, beautiful princesses, in beautiful dresses, diamonds, emeralds and pearls—"

"Are they true stories?"

I laughed. "No, but they *might* be."

"You hope they might be," she said. "I think these folk histories are like that."

Even after Aunt Mittie left for her home in Pickensville, I thought often of what she had said. I remembered the many times my sisters and I had been wandering in the woods from plum thicket to black-berry patches, and I had wondered if a certain briar patch hid Sleeping Beauty's castle. Or if one of the caves along the creek held bags of gold that had been hidden from the Yankees and forgotten. If the owner had been killed and nobody else knew where he'd hidden the fortune. Any wonderful thing could turn up when we set out on our foraging trips.

Was this what she meant?

And what about Mama's name for me?

Facing up to all this was painful and it didn't cure me completely of being a know-it-all. But it made me sometimes hold my tongue in situations where dreams were more important than facts.

11

Summer Nights after Supper

OUR FAVORITE TIMES WERE SUMMER nights after supper. Until cold weather came, we children spread quilts on the grass in the front yard and stretched out to watch the sky while Mama and Daddy, with any visiting kinfolks, sat around us in the dark rocking and talking.

The misty Milky Way was like a path across the sky. Constellations were hard to recognize but we could always find the Big Dipper. I had learned it pointed to the North Star that had been so important in history. On one of those nights I saw it for the first time. I expected the fabled North Star to be big and bright there in the northern sky. But it was so faint I could hardly see it. What a disappointment! We counted the shooting stars. In the fall there were showers of them.

Sometimes, to the northeast, the sky turned a hot red color. We knew that a steel mill furnace in Birmingham was pouring molten iron. The background music to those evenings was the steady call of the chuck-will's-widow from our woods and the faint blowing of a train whistle beyond the woods.

Even more entertaining than the sky and the night sounds were the stories the adults told, mostly family stories. My favorite was Daddy's adventure with the buzzard. At the time, around 1900, Oscar, my daddy, and his older brother Davis lived with their family at the Prude place, just outside Tuscaloosa.

The two boys saw town boys flying pretty, long-tailed kites in the March wind. It looked like such fun, and they longed for a big, bright kite with colored ribbons tied all the way down its long tail. But they lived on a farm growing cotton and hardly had food to eat. There was no money to buy play toys like kites.

Then calamity struck—one of the cows out in the pasture died. While their parents lamented the loss, Giles, their mother's youngest brother, made a joke of it. He was a fiddler and always spouting off verses. As he stood with Oscar and Davis watching the buzzards gliding into the pasture to feast on the dead cow, Giles danced a jig saying, "Ole cow died in the forks of the branch. The jaybirds whistled and the buzzards danced."

The boys, watching Giles and the buzzards dancing, got an idea. They set to work immediately. In a shack behind the house they found a strong box. They remembered that there was a long rope hanging on a nail in the barn, and in the woodpile there was a just-right stick. They lugged all this to the dead cow in the pasture. The buzzards took off to perch in trees around them and watch the work in progress.

The boys tied the rope to the stick and used it to prop up one side of the box over the cow body. Then they took their end of the rope into the nearby bushes. Soon the buzzards came winging back to the cow. They were so absorbed in feasting that they didn't notice the trap. The boys in the bushes watched tensely for the moment to spring their trap. That moment came when a buzzard fitted itself in the exact right position under the box. The boys jerked the rope, pulling the stick down and trapping the buzzard inside the box.

With a great flapping of wings, the other panic-stricken buzzards flew away while the boys rushed to the cow for their prisoner. It was flopping and struggling to escape but the well-built box held firm. Davis reached under to grab a buzzard leg, getting several sharp beak bites that made him holler. Oscar tied the rope securely around the buzzard's scaly leg. They tossed the box aside. And the boys had their kite! They held on to the rope and showed the scared buzzard how to run along the ground, letting it know it could take to the air. Soon it spread its wings, and went up, up, up. The pull on the rope was so strong that both boys had to grip it with all their might. The buzzard strained to go higher but the length of the rope hindered it.

The boys flew their kite all around the pasture whooping and laughing. Finally Oscar said, "Let's fly it up to the house and show them."

"Yeah, let's do. Won't they be surprised!"

When the boys came in sight of the house with their kite, the chickens began to stare and cackle. They ran squawking into the safety of the chicken house as the boys came closer. Buster, the dog, tucked his tail and ran under the house.

Sister Ruth hollered, "Mama! Papa! Come quick! Look what these boys have done now."

Their papa and Giles came from behind the house where they were cutting wood. Their mama hurried from the kitchen drying her hands on her apron. The other children ran from wherever they were. Everybody stared in amazement. Oscar and Davis soon realized, however, that they weren't pleased.

"Oh, boys!" their mama said in distress. "You've scared the hens so bad they'll stop laying. And what'll we do without eggs?"

"Take that filthy thing back to the pasture and let it go," their papa ordered.

Giles laughed so hard that he couldn't say anything. The brothers and sisters were wide-eyed. Little Nettie burst into tears and hid her face in their mama's skirt.

Ruth screamed. "It's puking on Davis! Ohhhh, how stinkin'." She held her nose and gagged.

"Hurry up!" their papa ordered. "Take it away and turn it loose."

Crestfallen, the boys flew their trophy back to the pasture. They pulled it down out of the sky. It bruised Oscar with its strong wings and ripped his hands with its beak while Davis untied the rope. The bird shot off and rose to the height of its brother birds circling the pasture.

The boys watched it go with regret. After putting their equipment away, they had to go to the creek to wash their clothes and themselves before they were allowed in the house. It was at least a week before Ruth stopped holding her nose whenever they came near her.

Our mama told interesting stories too, but they were different because she grew up in a small town on the Tombigbee River. Steamboats made two stops there, at the upper landing and the lower landing. Some of the boat captains would blow their whistles as they came to the first landing. The children would all run there and board the boat, and the captain would give them a free ride to the second landing where they got off. How exciting that must have been!

When Mama grew older, the crowd of young folks, including Mama and several of her cousins, would gather at one of their houses to sit on the porch and the steps, planning.

"It's such a pretty night let's go serenading," a boy suggested one evening.

Everybody agreed. The boys got their instruments—mandolins, fiddles, banjos, and guitars. Then they walked all over town playing, singing, and visiting at each house. The people brought out whatever treats they had—cake, homemade wine, parched peanuts, candy. Usually the jolly group was out till one o'clock in the morning.

Sometimes the boys took chickens to Miss Annie Sanders's house and she'd turn them into a feast of chicken and dumplings for the serenaders to sit round her table and enjoy. My mouth watered as I listened to this story. We had eaten plain cornbread crumbled in buttermilk for supper.

Jane said wistfully, "But nobody has enough chickens now to do that."

None of us added that we had no musical instruments, and couldn't play them if we did. No cousins lived anywhere near us and our only friends were school friends. There was no way we could go serenading.

We children all agreed we'd like to have belonged to Mama's serenaders and enjoyed all that food and socializing, but Daddy's adventure was the most fun.

12

The Howton Horror

EARLY ONE SUMMER MORNING I took a bucket of feed downhill to the pasture expecting to find our teenage calves, Skinny Dugin and Rose, waiting for me as usual. I saw Skinny, a handsome Guernsey, standing at the gate. But where was black-and-white Rose?

As I trotted closer I spotted Rose lying down in the edge of the grass. I fed Skinny Dugin and scratched her hornless head. Rose made no move to join us though she was always hungry for breakfast. Was she sick? I hurried over to her. Right away I saw that her black nose was bloody. Looking closer, I saw blood oozing from three deep scratches about an inch apart. They went upward, then down the length of Rose's back, three deep claw marks. Under her neck was more blood. Some varmint had attacked Rose! And not long ago because the blood hadn't dried. I ran to the house for Mama. She'd just started breakfast but she dropped everything and we ran back to Rose.

"What a fight she had," Mama said after examining her. "Let's get her up to see if she's hurt otherwise."

We helped Rose stand. She was able to walk and began eating her breakfast. I noticed our neighbor, Mr. Givens, and another man in the lane that led to the highway. They were looking at something on the ground.

"I believe that's Mr. Raines with him," Mama said. "He's the oldest man in Brookwood. Run see if he'll come look at Rose."

I ran downhill and climbed the fence. The two men were measuring something. After we good-morninged each other I told them about Rose.

"Well, see here," Mr. Givens said after I finished. "These big tracks. They's three toes on each foot and the hind tracks are six feet from the front ones. Some big critter's been along this road not a long time back."

They followed me to Rose and looked her over.

"These are the same as the three claws in the tracks," Mr. Raines finally said. "But I never saw anything like it."

"I'd guess a painter," Mr. Givens said, "but none o' them's left in this country, not since my grandpa's day."

"This is not like what I've heard tell of panthers, though," Mr. Raines said. "It's a wonder this yearling got away."

"Didn't you hear anything?" Mama asked Mr. Givens.

"Naw. And if Addie heered anything she'da woke me." He spat tobacco juice on a bitterweed. "I'm jist as glad she didn't. I wouldn'ta wanted to meet that thing in the dark. Or anytime."

Later that day, when I was at the mailbox, I saw Archie, Francys's classmate from Howton, coming from the Brookwood store with a sack of flour on his shoulder. I waved at him, and he hollered, "I heard them talking at the store about what happened to your yearlings."

I waited, anxious to tell him all about it.

He laid his bag of flour across the mailbox to rest his arms, and listened. Afterward he said. "Did you hear what happened to me?"

I shook my head no, big-eyed.

"Sunday night I was coming home from church, walking through the woods without a light but I know the way by heart. It was about eleven o'clock and I wasn't in a hurry, but I began hearing something, some kind of noise that told me I'd better get in a hurry. It was following me and it was laughing and growling and sort of chittering. I geared up faster, began running and it did too. I never was so glad to see anything as I was to see our yard gate. I didn't bother to open it—I just jumped over." He paused, breathing hard. "It scares me now just thinking about it."

"Where were your dogs?"

"On the porch, their heads up, listening, but they wouldn't stir. I was gonna sic 'em on the thing but they wouldn't budge."

"Could you see it?"

"Just enough to tell it was big." He shuddered. "Dark's not gonna catch me in the woods again."

"Did you look for tracks?"

"In the woods that way it didn't leave any tracks."

I offered to show him the tracks in the Givenses' lane but he hefted the bag of flour onto his shoulder. "I better get on down the road. Miz Lambert sent Ma some buttermilk and she wants to make biscuits for supper."

I understood. He had two more miles to go. Besides I was in a hurry to get up the lane to our house and spread his news.

Before dark came I brought Rose and Skinny Dugin into the safety of the barn. That night I lay awake a long time imagining the big thing coming after Archie in the dark making those odd noises. Could it be what attacked Rose? But if it ate calves, why would it want to catch a human? I said my prayers all over again, thanking God for saving Rose and that she and Skinny Dugin were safe tonight. I had said my "Amen" before I remembered to thank Him for saving Archie so I added a postscript.

A week passed without us hearing any more till Sunday when Mary Alice brought Lizabeth home with her from church. At the dinner table Lizabeth was ready to tell us the latest because it involved her.

"You know a protracted meeting's going on at the Chigger Ridge Church. Well, I spent the night with Bertha and she wanted to go. After church we got a ride as far as the Howton store. But then we had to walk and we didn't have no light. I was scared but Bertha said there wadn't any truth to those tales the boys have been telling and we'd just go right on. She dared that ole booger to get us—he'd be sorry." She paused to gnaw on a fried chicken leg and take a drink of iced tea. "We hadn't got far in those dark woods before I was ready to go back. She wouldn't hear it though—called me a poltroon, whatever that is, like a coward maybe—and we kept plodding on. But when the noises started she forgot that bragging talk quick enough." She glanced around the table and said, "Thank you for another biscuit and that bowl of squash."

"Don't be so slow," I said, passing her the bowls.

"What kind of noises?" Francys asked.

"Laughing, but like a crazy laugh. And it wadn't trying to creep up on us. It was banging and knocking through the woods like it couldn't see good." She chewed awhile. "When I looked back I could see it was big"—she stretched the word out—"like a big ole dog in a hurry on his hind legs, and a-talking and laughing to hisself. I tell you it was a fright. I froze in my tracks. Bertha grabbed my hand and said, 'Let's go!' dragging me with her. But I can't run like that. I clutched my side and hollered after Bertha, 'Slow down. Remember my bad heart.' You know what that hateful girl hollered back at me? 'Your bad heart, hell. I'm gone from here.' And she disappeared. I'm telling you true—that girl Bertha, coming from church, cussed!"

Daddy laughed. "Seems to me it was time for a little cussing."

"Well, I chased after her but got tangled in a vine and fell. I rolled myself into the bushes. That thing went thundering past. I lay there scared silly hoping it would catch that Bertha and tote her off. After everything was quiet I went creeping through the woods to Bertha's house. She was in the yard with her pa trying to get the dogs out from under the house. They had good sense and wouldn't come."

By this time Mama was serving the huckleberry cobbler with refills on the ice tea.

Lizabeth didn't slow down. "Now this evening I'm going to see Aunt Tood—you know she's Pa's ancestor, older than Methuselah. Pa says she might know something about this Horror."

"Where's your Aunt Tood now?" Mama asked.

"She's in Ina Mae's rest home there on the highway. You know, Ina Mae's house where she keeps old people. Y'all wanna go with me?" She waved her spoon at Mary Alice and me. I was ready. But Mary Alice objected to the long, hot walk and stayed at home.

Right after dinner Lizabeth and I set out. Mama saw us to the door with the warning, "Don't accept any rides from anybody. Don't get in anybody's car, you hear?" We heard. It was easy to obey her as not many cars passed us on the road. One tooted his horn as he passed but we wouldn't look.

At Ina Mae's we went into the long back room with lots of windows. Beds of old ladies, about three feet apart, filled it. Aunt Tood wasn't asleep and she was eager to talk about the Horror, as she called it. "That thang comes back ever' so often. We wuz always skeered of it but it never stayed long. Just passin' through, y'know. When my chillun wuz little we lived over toward the river, back of beyond, you might say. One night after supper the little ones wuz playing out in the yard. I heard that thang squalling through the woods. Law! It made my hair rise up stiff. The kids all run for the porch. I got them inside and we locked the door. But the mules knew it wuz lurkin' around. We had them quartered under the house to keep folks from stealing 'em. All night long they'd blow their lips and stomp their feet letting us know something was out there. But we never ventured outside."

"Did you ever see it?" I asked.

"No, not nare time that it came. We didn't want to see it."

After we left Aunt Tood, Lizabeth and I parted. She went to her home and I hightailed it for mine. But what do you know—there came Otis's mama. Her house was in the strip mine pit so I had to take time to ask her about the monster.

"Well," she said, "one night I'd gone to bed. Otis'd promised to come home early but you know how boys are. He fooled around with those Puzak boys, and it was plumb dark when he started home. I was sound asleep when I heard him a-hollerin' like a stuck pig. 'Mama, open the door! Open the door, Mama!' and he was crashing through the woods like a mad bull. Before I could get the door open, he hit the porch running and dragged me with him back in the house and slammed the door and locked it. He couldn't say a word, he was so wrung out. I brung him a glass of water to help calm him. 'That thang wanted to get me, Mama. It was right on my duster.' 'What, what?' I asked him. 'Like a huge, big gorilla thang up on its hind legs, a-laughin' and mutterin' and running fast as a motorcar. Mama, it nearly got me.' I had to make that big ole boy a pallet on the floor in my room before he'd go to bed." Otis's mama went on her way.

After that things quieted down. When fall began Mr. Raines

showed up to ask about Rose. I was glad I could say she was healed.

"I believe the thing's gone," he said. "Nobody's heard of it lately. It must be getting old, probably toothless now and going hungry. It may not come again."

I was sorry. Knowing that it could be lurking about the settlements put ginger in my routine days. Still I never let dark catch me in the woods. It just might come back again.

13

Shangri-La

TOWARD THE END OF SUMMER life got sort of boring—crops laid by, no kinfolks visiting, no books or magazines to read. Sometimes I'd take the fly swatter to the front porch and kill flies.

An interesting thing I had discovered was smashing a fly didn't kill it. As it lay there, no longer in the shape of a fly, several of its brother flies would gather round it and begin pumping life back into it. Before long the fly body would be back on its feet and ready to fly away. I could never get over the marvel of it.

Another pastime I had discovered was catching hummingbirds. I'd become famous for capturing those darting, swift-flying beauties as none of the other children could do it. When I captured a rubythroat in midair I thrilled to the miracle of holding that tiny living jewel in my hands. I was very tender with all I caught, letting them loose after Mama admired them. One time another hummer that looked bigger and plainer than the rubythroats landed in front of me on the wire fence. As I moved my hands toward it, it did not fly away, but gripped the wire fence tighter and opened its long, sharp beak as wide as possible and screamed and screamed. That one too I showed to Mama then released.

Catching a june bug and tying a thread to a hind leg was another pastime of desperation. We children would fly the green-gold bugs around like miniature kites. Though june bugs too were beautiful, they left a rancid odor on our hands after we let them go.

On a day when Daddy was at home, an exciting break came in the monotonous days—he and Mama decided to haul our two young calves to the wild area beyond the old Lawrence place and turn them loose to spend the rest of the summer browsing. Modestine, named for Robert Louis Stevenson's donkey, was already over there. We also needed to see about her and take her a bucket of feed.

Daddy dragged out the back seat of our Model A Ford. I spread sheets of newspaper on the floor—sometimes the little fellows got carsick—and put in an upturned bucket for me to sit on. My job was to comfort and control the calves as they took the second car ride of their lives—their first one was when we brought them home from the dairy.

Not only was it wild over beyond the Lawrence place but the logging road was washed out and rough. At an abandoned hut we parked and got out. There was not a sound in the thick green forest. Mama began calling, "Sookie, Modestine, suuuuuukkk." I joined in and shortly we heard something big hurrying through the brush. Out of the thick greenery burst Modestine looking well and glad to see us and especially the bucket of sweet feed.

"She's in good shape," Mama said. "And there're not many ticks on her."

Daddy was checking her feet. "Her hooves are okay," he said. "Let's unload the young ones now. We want them to know that they belong together."

We lifted the calves out, petted them, and gave them some of the feed. The three of them looked like kinfolks. They were all a rich tan color with some white on their backs—Guernsey. I curried Modestine and picked off ticks. Mama and Daddy went to check on the spring behind the hut to make sure the water was flowing for them.

We left the calves together, hoping they would be safe till late fall when we'd return to bring them home for winter. As we drove away I kept looking back, thinking I must feel like parents do when their child first leaves home.

"Mr. Fred Criss lives somewhere in here," I heard Daddy say. "I'd like to go by and see him a minute if we can find him."

We found his home in a valley secluded by pine-covered hills. I stopped still holding my breath, just looking. Beautiful, peaceful, shut away from the world, a place where no one ever grew old.

"Shangri-La!" I thought. "This must be it." The sun was setting behind the hills. A layer of blue smoke hung among the big pines that made the air fresh and cool. Shed needles covered the ground with a thick blanket of straw. We could hardly see the house, it was so smothered in growing things. The yard overflowed with blossoms. Mama and I began naming them.

"Four-o'clocks," I said. "And look at all the different colors on one bush."

"Dwarf lilacs and periwinkles," Mama pointed out. "But I don't recognize these little orange blooms with the lacy leaves."

"Our red cannas are pretty," I said, "but look at these yellow ones sprinkled with red dots. And bachelor buttons and nasturtiums." I remembered nasturtiums because I used to chew the leaves, and I knew their name meant "nose twister" because of their zingy odor. We saw green, fragrant sage, dill, basil, wild bergamot, and other herbs that I just had to squeeze the leaves to smell.

"In all this I'll bet he has that flower my mother grew in her garden at Pickensville," Mama said. "'Shower of diamonds' she called it. Such an unusual flower." But, hard as we searched, we couldn't recognize anything that looked like a shower of diamonds.

Daddy found Mr. Criss hoeing sweet potatoes which seemed to be growing everywhere. He was glad to see us. So was his knee-high dog, Bill, whose fluffy black-and-white coat was well combed. Bill followed at my heels as we toured the grounds. The okra was so high that I had to look up to see the top, and the cotton was taller than Daddy. Every growing thing went about its business with enthusiasm. We passed a wild-looking calf with shaggy ears as long as a burro's. He kindly permitted me to pat him. An old broken-down wagon leaned against a pine tree in front of the house like what you see in a painting of life out west. My fingers yearned to capture it in my drawing book. At the edge of the yard was a clear spring that bubbled out of the ground with the same gusto as everything else.

We followed a neat brick walk curving up to his porch where we sat awhile. Mama and I complimented him on his gorgeous flowers. He said he liked to collect wild flowers when he was going through the woods.

"Have you ever been to the old Williams place?" he asked. "It's on this side of the creek. An old log house that's just about gone. Nobody lives there now, but that's where you should go to see wild flowers. In spring the Easter lilies cover the floor of the woods like a carpet—white, pale yeller, and pinkish. Some folks call them rain lilies—dunno why." Then he added, "Nobody goes there much anymore, claim it's haunted. And that may be."

Which led him to tell us how he would stretch out on a rag rug in front of his fire in winter and listen to wild horse spirits running through the woods neighing.

"Don't you get scared?" I asked.

"Naw, they don't scare me. I never heard of a haint hurting any-body." I was silent as I was not familiar with the habits of haints.

"When I was a boy," he continued, "I wanted to someday be a doc-tor. One summer I set myself up in business. All of us boys went bare-footed, and we all got dew poison, the toe itch. You ain't never had an itch till you've had the toe itch. It's plum pure misery. I was struck by an idee. I picked all the cayenne peppers out of the garden and boiled them into a powerful potion. Then I told the boys to come to my house and I'd sure relieve their suffering. They flocked to our porch and waited in line while I took them one by one to a back room. There I'd be real official and have the patient hold up his cracked, swollen, and raw toes. After my inspection, and a little hemming and hawing, I'd swab his feet with my red cayenne pepper concoction. In the minute it took for him to realize what was happening I hustled him out the back door and shut it tight. While I went to the front porch for the next pa-tient, I heard the one on the back porch going mad, stomping on the floorboards and yelping, finally jumping to the ground and running screaming into the woods." He laughed. "The ailing boy traded one torture for another but at least he forgot his unbearable itch. And the funny thing was boys kept coming to me for my cure."

Dark was moving softly through the trees. I heard a birdsong, just three notes like a flute. "A wood thrush," Daddy said. "I haven't heard one since I was a boy."

"Earlier today a rain crow was calling up the rain," Mr. Criss said.

I couldn't see Mama in the shadows. "We sure need a good soaking rain," she said. "Everything's drying up. Did you ever see a rain crow?"

"Nope. They're a real timid bird. A good hider."

"They're really a cuckoo," Daddy said. "But not destructive like some cuckoos. I could never sight one either."

The time had come to say goodbye. "I hope I can find my way out of here," Daddy said, shaking hands with Mr. Criss.

"You can," he replied. "I see you got a good helper here." He grinned at me.

For the rest of the summer I had no trouble with boredom. I thought about that lush, secluded valley so hidden by hills and forests, and hoped that Mr. Criss had finally sighted the elusive rain crow. I thought about our young calves that had taken such a big step out into the world and were learning from Modestine how to be proper cows. And I worked in the pages of my drawing book trying to capture with my pencil what I saw on our visit to Shangri-La.

14

Aileen Falls by the Wayside

MOST DAYS IN SUMMER I felt well. I was wiry as a half-starved young goat and just as active. I spent most mornings, from about seven o'clock on, down in the grassy pasture watching Annie the cow graze and keeping her from straying into the cornfield. I thought of myself as Heidi, the girl in the Swiss Alps who herded goats with Peter and had adventures. The only thing was, I never had adventures. Sometimes people passed by in the distance, on the lane that led to Mr. Givens's house and to the Quarters where Aunt Janie and her husband Mr. Will lived, but nobody ever came close enough to talk to me.

Then one day I realized I was sick. My right eye hurt me most painfully and I couldn't hold it open because of the bright sunlight. Worst of all, because of the pain, I couldn't read anything. I kept my head down when I was with anyone or else turned my face away, hoping nobody would notice and the ailment would go away. I should have known I couldn't escape Mama's sharp eyes.

She said to Daddy, "You need to look at Aileen's eye. I think it's infected."

Daddy had me come to the front porch where the light was good and sit on a brick half column made to hold a big Boston fern except we didn't have any ferns. He studied my eye for a long while then sighed.

"Yes," he said to Mama. "We've got to get her to a doctor."

There was the dilemma. We were living through an especially rocky time that summer of 1935 when our car was broken down and we had no money to fix it. And where would we find an eye doctor? If we found one, how would I get to him? How would we pay him? Little did we suspect that this dilemma would set our feet on a long path that would eventually give us a battle cry to help overcome the hardships of the Great Depression.

Daddy thought about what to do all night long. At breakfast he said, "I remember hearing about an old-time eye doctor named Searcy in Tuscaloosa. We'll have to thumb a ride and see if he'll check her eye."

I took a "bird bath" in the wash pan and put on a dress, a rose-pink, silky one Aunt Martha had sent from Pittsburgh. I wore Francys's shoes as I didn't have any. By eight o'clock Daddy and I were standing on the side of the road. He raised his thumb at every car that came around the curve going toward Tuscaloosa. None of them even paused as they passed us by.

"Ah," Daddy said after an hour or so. "Here comes Mr. Benton. He'll be going to town." And he stepped onto the edge of the road, raised his thumbing arm, and looked hopefully into the oncoming car. But, like the others, it passed right on by without hesitating.

"He was all by himself too," I said. "He had lots of room for us."

By dinnertime we were both hot and thirsty and our stomachs were telling us it had been five hours since we'd eaten, so we decided to give up.

"It's too late anyway," Daddy said. "The doctor's office would probably be closed by the time we got there. And we'd be caught in town after dark without a way home."

Mama had cooked some turnip greens from the garden and made hot water cornbread. With a tasty onion, and buttermilk to drink, we feasted.

I took off my dress, folded it carefully for another try tomorrow, and gave Francys back her shoes. Then I spent the rest of the day in a dark room. Everybody else was busy doing chores, which I should have been helping with, but I knew I was on the sidelines for the time being. I could tell by the sounds what was happening. Francys was washing the dishes, Jane was sweeping the floors, Mama was churning the clabbered milk to make butter and buttermilk, and Mary Alice was filling a bucket of water to take to Daddy who was working in the field. I heard my little brother outside playing under the privet hedge.

This day set the pattern for the days to come. When I did get to the doctor he said I had a dendritic ulcer. He explained it was an ulcer that spread in my eye like tree branches. He had to see me at least two days a week, and every time he explained carefully what he was doing to try to treat the ulcer. One time he thought malaria might be causing it so I took doses of quinine. Another time he scraped my eye and applied iodine. It burned like fire. He wanted me to continue staying in a dark room every day. Only after sunset could I come outside for a walk.

Daddy couldn't make appointments because he never knew if we could get a ride or not. But Dr. Searcy didn't quibble about taking me whenever I could come. He was a small man, cheery, quick moving, and plainspoken—nothing fancy about him or his gloomy rooms with their dark wood walls, glass-enclosed bookcases holding thick dark books, and stiff, uncomfortable, dark leather chairs. Everything looked as if it had been in place for the last hundred years.

Usually I had a long wait because the waiting room was always crowded, mostly with country people like me. As I couldn't look at the magazines, I entertained myself studying the people, eavesdropping on their conversations, and speculating about some of the drivers who picked us up. One thirtyish man, driving an open Packard-type car very fast, especially fascinated me. I had sat in the back seat behind Daddy. The dark glasses I wore allowed me to watch the man's eyes reflected in the rearview mirror—fierce looking, intent on the road, under heavy black brows. I wondered why such a man would pick us up as he didn't seem to feel kindly toward us. Daddy made some pleasant remarks but the man wasn't chatty so Daddy soon kept quiet. By the time we reached town, I was whipped into a frazzle by the speed and the wind, and my hair was standing on end. With few words and no change of expression, the man put us out in Tuscaloosa and continued on his way west.

While I spent my time in the doctor's waiting room, Daddy walked the long way from Sixth Street through town and down River Hill to Stallworth Lake where the Relief Office was. He was asking for help paying my doctor bill and for the medicines I had to have. He always came back discouraged. After that, he had to go down to the Yellow

Front Store, where country people hung out, and try to find us a ride home. As there were two of us, it was harder to find a way. We were grateful to ride in the back of pickups, coal trucks, cars without floors so that I could see the road passing under us—we were glad for any free thing on wheels that went our way.

Finally, something the doctor did helped my eye, but the ulcer left a white scar over my brown pupil. It was like I was seeing through a heavy fog. Now I had to have glasses—another expense when every penny counted. I noticed with anxiety that Daddy was growing slower and more stooped, and Mama was more uptight and anxious. I couldn't think what to do to help. With the many medical bills, on top of the grocery bills and animal feed bills at the Brookwood store, the anxiety in our family increased. Daddy wore out several sets of dimestore shoe sole kits walking the highway to Birmingham in search of work. We sold our cow. We sold the old sow. We ate most of our chickens, keeping just a few laying hens so we could have eggs for breakfast.

In September no rains came, our garden dried up, and we had to sell the few hens that remained. There was nothing left in our kitchen cupboard for the seven of us.

"I'll have to go back to the Relief Office," Daddy said. "If they'll just give us a little food to tide us over till I can find some kind of work . . ."

"I know it's hard," Mama said. "They're all city people with degrees from the university. They don't know how it is out here in the country. And they think we have too many children."

"The worse thing is they make a fellow feel so no-count," Daddy said.

As he stood by the roadside thumbing, I could see how he dreaded to face Miss Johnson and Mr. Allen, the ones he always had to explain to. We could visualize Miss Johnson—blonde hair drawn back smoothly like Ann Harding, the movie star, glacial blue-gray eyes, and a patrician profile. Daddy had never seen her smile. Mr. Allen was her male counterpart.

Daddy was gone all day. In the twilight after chores were done, we gathered on the front porch watching the highway anxiously. Would Daddy catch a ride home or was he walking the eighteen miles?

At last a coal truck stopped at the end of our lane and Daddy got out. He came slowly up the hill walking as if his bones hurt. He was not carrying anything, not a bag or a box, nothing. We waited on the porch, stricken.

"Didn't they give you *anything?*" Mama asked when he reached the steps.

"Come in the kitchen," he said.

We followed him and stood around the table in suspense while he struggled to get something out of his pocket. He laid it on the table—a waif of a cabbage the size of his fist with yellow, worm-eaten outer leaves. We stared.

My daddy was not a cusser. But he blistered the silence with "Hot dog ole man Allen!"

Every one of us burst out in a roar of laughter. We laughed until some of us cried. And cried. And cried.

We had cabbage for supper that night though there were hardly two tablespoons for each of us. And it was tasty. As Mama said, "Cabbage is cabbage no matter how old and shriveled it is. But maybe next time they'll give you a bag to put it in."

We had more tense times ahead of us, but whenever we were most desperate, one of us intoned, "Hot dog ole man Allen!" and we all laughed and took heart again.

The Relief Office never knew it, but they gave us something more valuable than an overage cabbage—a battle cry to keep up the struggle till we finally won.

15

A Visit From the Detroit Cousins

WHEN THE BIG, DUSTY BLACK car came bumping up our lane that
summer day in 1936 we all ran to meet it. Before the car stopped, the
doors burst open and out leaped James Hunter, Mabel Grace, Charles
David, Boots, and Alfred. Aunt Bessie took longer, unkinking her
neck, stretching her legs, and flexing her driving arms. It was a long
way from Detroit, Michigan, to Brookwood, Alabama, especially when
you couldn't afford to stop overnight at a tourist court. Our bond with
these city cousins was our memory of the old mining camp, Cedar
Cove, and the time before the mine closed when, as far as we were
concerned, all was right with the world.

While Mama took Aunt Bessie to the kitchen for iced tea, the rest
of us unloaded the car and helped the boys settle in the back bedroom
where they would stay with their mother. Jane, Francys, Mabel, and
Boots were to stay with Mary Alice and me in our one room upstairs.
To make space for all of them, I had crowded my treasures under my
bed and on the sills of my half of the ten windows. Our plan was for
two to sleep in each double bed and two on a pallet on the floor. But as
it turned out, when the nights were clear some of us took pallets to the
front porch. That was the best. Jack, our collie, liked having our company too. Our little brother, Buddy, slept in the front bedroom with
Mama and Daddy.

That first morning of their visit I was up before sunrise and out
with my scythe to cut an armload of grass for Annie, our milk cow. I
didn't want to miss a minute of the day after everybody else was up.

When I came back to the house Mama already had a fire in the cook-stove, the oatmeal was simmering, and Daddy was ready to leave for work. Mama was in the barn milking.

Our three baby calves were in an uproar, butting the walls of their stall and bawling, demanding that Mama hurry up with their break-fast. One calf belonged to our cow Annie. James Hunter appeared in time to help me turn her in with Annie after Mama finished milking. Greedy little soul that she was, she hunched her mother with such de-termination to make her give down more milk that Annie staggered as she tried to eat the grass I'd brought her.

I had taught the other two calves to drink their milk from a bucket. They were orphans from a Tuscaloosa dairy. James couldn't believe that we got boy calves for free and paid only one dollar for each girl calf. I was tickled to show him how they gobbled their milk and how satisfied they were afterward.

Charles David was up in time to help Mama feed the chickens. He fell in love with them right away. I watched him in the chicken yard while James Hunter and I picked figs for breakfast. He sat on an old log with the hens gathered round him, red, white, black, and speckled. He petted them and talked to them and beamed at the way they talked back to him.

During breakfast we decided to go blackberry picking so we could have a cobbler for dinner.

"You kids watch for snakes," Aunt Bessie warned. "Snakes like to hide in berry bushes."

"I think those scare stories are made up," Mama said. "No snake would climb over those bramble briars—they're too stickery. But be alert anyway."

Francys laughed as we went banging and hollering out the door with our buckets. "I think that bunch would scare any snake to death."

It was a good blackberry year and we remembered where our best picking had been last year. Shiny blackberries big as nickels needed just a little nudge to drop into our buckets. Our picking rules allowed the picker to eat all he or she wanted so plenty of eating went on. When the sun got high and hot we combined what we'd picked into two buckets, judging that would be enough for a huge pie and started for home. It was farther than we thought. We were sweating and the bugs were biting and our legs didn't want to go. But later, when we were eating that juicy, ruby-red-and-black pie with Mama's butter crust, we forgot how we'd suffered.

Another day we toured the wild plum thickets and did see a snake, a beautiful one that was striped and spotted. The cousins picked up rocks and sticks to kill it because it looked at us with an evil eye, they said. Mary Alice and I held out against them while the snake lay there in the grass waiting for us to go on about our business.

"It eats the bad snakes," I argued. "Mama watched one in our field swallow a rattler twice as big as it was."

"How can it do that?" Mabel doubted.

"Somehow its jaws come unhinged, Mama said. She has a pet snake that lives in a corner of our garden, a puffing adder."

So the snake was saved and we moved on to another plum thicket. From that trip we took every bucket home full of plump red, pink, and yellow plums, enough for eating and several jars of jam.

One morning Liza brought a message from Mrs. Smith saying she had loads of pears that needed picking. We got our buckets, climbed the stile into the Smiths' cornfield, and followed Liza to the pear trees. James Hunter ate more than he picked. Before we got back home, he was so sticky with sweet pear juice that it seemed the flies were trying to tote him off. Mama added pear salad with grated cheese and candied red cherries to the dinner menu.

One of our longest food adventures was hiking through the woods to Chigger Ridge to buy okra and field peas from Miz Price. The many children in that house interested us but all we did was sit on the floor of their front room and look at each other. Their house was almost bare of furniture. Mama and Miz Price sat in two straight chairs, the only chairs we saw, and talked about their gardens. Mabel began wiggling and finally whispered, "Chiggers are biting me." I knew that wasn't so as the chiggers hadn't had time to find a good biting place on her. But she went out in the yard to wait for us. We straggled home loaded with peas, okra, summer squash, and cucumbers. Sitting in the shade under the chinaberry tree, we shelled peas while Mama made cornbread.

Cornbread was James Hunter's joy. As soon as it came out of the oven in Grandmother's iron pans he sat at the table and ate crusty muffins and corn sticks, spreading some with mustard and some with butter. Stuffed, he left the kitchen to stretch out on the shady front porch and digest.

When a lightning storm came up, we closed the doors at each end of the long hall and sat on the lower stairsteps while Mabel, up on the platform for a stage, sang one song after the other. We didn't know any of them as we didn't have a radio, but in the dark there we couldn't see the lightning and could barely hear the thunder so we all felt safer.

The kind of songs we knew were on the old records stored in the Victrola that Mama had earned selling from the Larkin catalog at Cedar Cove—"The Prisoner's Song," "Where Is My Wandering Boy Tonight," "Mother, Put My Little Shoes Away." The Victrola was a floor model, stained mahogany with a golden arm, a fancy sound box, and a roomy record cabinet. Maybe I cranked it too tight, or overworked it, but one day I was playing "The Gypsy's Warning" when, from deep inside, it gave a sudden prolonged roar that nearly knocked James out of his chair, and then stopped stone still. Nothing we did brought it back to life. From that day on we had only Mabel for our music.

After a storm we went to the big spring to play in the swollen branch. Charles David and I dug gray clay out of the bank and sculpted people's heads and whole animals. He tried to shape a chicken with little success. Jane and James Hunter didn't appreciate our art. They sat on a log and discussed Life. Though James and I were the same age, he was much more worldly-wise.

The cousins wanted to educate us to some of their Detroit ways. Besides Mabel's songs and James Hunter's man-of-the-world stories, they tried to teach us some foreign sounding words and phrases that they said would get us killed if we said them on the streets up there. We weren't motivated to learn as we weren't interested in getting killed in Detroit or anywhere else.

Every night Aunt Bessie lined up all ten of us and sprayed our throats with something she said would keep us from getting infantile paralysis, or polio, the disease that paralyzed so many, even President Roosevelt, and killed thousands of people.

When we were at home during the day our hill rocked with chasing, yelling, fussing, and fighting. Our most played game, something we called "crazy woman," combined all these activities. Charles David was not often involved with us. He preferred associating with the chickens. Mama depended on him to help her keep them watered and fed and to gather the eggs every day.

A gang of kids overeating watermelon, stuffing themselves on wild plums, and gulping down unpeeled peaches and wormy apples kept our tack-and-hammered-on privy busy. It was down the hill from the house, and nobody suspected danger lurked there till the day a cloud of furious yellow jackets chased Charles David, bawling and half-dressed, up the hill. A loud outcry with Detroit accents went up to burn the privy down, but soon everybody realized we couldn't do without it. When Daddy came home that night he and Mama disposed of the yellow jackets.

On an all-day expedition with no purpose, we went to the trestle beyond the big spring. After waving the train past we crossed the high trestle where we were even with the birds in the treetops. We walked into the Howton woods, thick with big trees and bushes. Some of them I couldn't recognize. We heard the rushing murmur of the waterfall before we came in sight of it.

No matter how often I saw it, I was always transfixed at its beauty, the water dropping all that way down into a deep pool that was surrounded by lacy ferns and dwarf irises. We sat to rest and look with wondering eyes at the steep wooded hills piled with huge rocks. Great clumps of pink-blossomed mountain laurel grew among rock piles. Tall slim cowcumbers were in bloom, their huge white flowers smelling like sweet lemons.

The rest of us explored and collected while James went swimming in the clear waterfall pool. Waxy white Indian pipes caught my eye and beside them I found a petrified unicorn horn. With a thrill, I showed it to the others.

"It looks more like a rhinoceros horn to me," Boots said.

"When have you seen a rhinoceros?" I asked defensively.

"In the zoo," she said.

Since I'd never been to a zoo I couldn't dispute her, but it stayed a unicorn horn for me.

We started home heavy laden but nobody could part with a thing. Hot and weary, we finally came out of the woods and saw our house in the distance. A chain gang was working on the road but we wouldn't look as we passed for fear of embarrassing them. Chained together in the sun and wearing their black-and-white-striped prison uniforms, they were hotter and more exhausted than we were, I knew. But I did look at their guard. He was young and round faced, with silver-rimmed eyeglasses and a big gun. He was smiling, not at us but about us.

How glad we were to get all of our findings home safe. We ate a whole loaf of bread spread with peanut butter and a basket of plump red tomatoes that James and I went to the garden and picked.

Then we sat on the front porch to wait for the mailman. We expected a free sample of Ex-Lax that we had ordered with a penny postcard the week before. We recognized the mailman's car when it turned onto our road. But he came too slow, taking forever at each mailbox. A chant went up on the porch: "C'mon, slowpoke. Shake a leg, dumbbell." But we soon regretted our calls to hurry because he brought a letter from Bessie's husband, Uncle Charley, saying they should come home. A loud groan went up. Everybody wanted to stay another week but Aunt Bessie decreed they had to leave the next day. And so they did.

Charles David begged to stay. "Mama, I'll come home later on the bus. It just costs five dollars. Please. Please . . ." When she wouldn't relent he sat on the front porch rocking and looking at the floor.

The day after they left, our sample of Ex-Lax came. I opened it standing at the mailbox.

The chocolate I saw meant candy to me. I ate it all, much to my regret later.

The next week from Detroit Mama received a letter:

> *Dear Aunt Gertrude We got home Saturday at 6 o'clock. I am not having as much fun as we did their. I wish I was there with you. I*

wish I was there feen the chickens. But I will be back summer take care of our chickens Your Nephew Charles Cox.

But he never came back. Mama and the chickens pined for him while life went on for the rest of us.

16

The KKK Checks Up on Big Hurricane Baptist

AT FIRST THAT SUNDAY NIGHT in 1936 seemed no different from our usual Sunday nights. After supper I fed Jack and the cats, then Daddy and I set off in his pickup in time to get to church before anyone else came. We turned on the lights, raised the windows to let in the cooler air from the creek, picked up litter left behind from the morning service, and replaced the ragged hymnals in the racks on the back of each bench.

Brother Neale arrived, moving slowly after making his three-mile walk to the church for the second time that day, and sat beside the pulpit turning the pages of his Bible. His sermon messages seldom varied, but oh, his prayers were like poetry addressed to God. Our Sunday night attendance was always less than the morning service. There were fewer children for one thing, and some adults who had radios preferred to stay home and listen to their favorite programs.

With the peppy opening hymn, "Revive Us Again," I chose a seat near the back. That way in case someone new came in I could welcome them. This almost never happened, but just in case it did, I was there. Brother Neale had finished his pre-sermon prayer on his knees and now stepped toward the pulpit when I noticed an unusual quiet outside the church. Those men and boys who never came inside for the service but looked through the windows, smoking and discussing what we were doing—their voices were all silent.

Then I heard many muffled car doors closing and some sort of movement toward the steps like an invasion coming. I turned to look at the door. The knob twisted, and the door quietly swung open. Looking in, surveying members and how they were spaced about, was a figure dressed in a white robe and a white peaked cap that covered his face. For one second through the slits in the mask I saw the dark glitter of his eyes. This was not the kind of new visitor I had expected to greet. I didn't stir—I couldn't. The white figure stepped inside and stood beside a back pew. He was followed by so many robed, peaked figures that I lost count. He remained standing until they were all in place, then they sat as one man. They made no unnecessary movements and almost no sound.

Brother Neale hadn't noticed them, probably because of his failing eyesight and hearing. Not one of the congregation moved after that first look. It was as if we were frozen in place. During the sermon we were as still as the men in white but I doubt that we heard anything the preacher said. I know that I didn't. When we stood for the closing prayer, the man who had come in first walked down the center aisle with a small but heavy-looking bag in his gloved hand. He placed it on the pulpit. I strained my ears, but as far as I could hear, he said nothing. He turned without hurry to go out the door, followed slowly and quietly by the rest of them.

All of us stood listening till the last of their cars drove away. Then with a gasping breath we rushed to the front to gather around our preacher. He emptied the bag on the straight chair beside him. What a pile of silver money! More than I had seen in my entire fifteen years. No wonder that bag had looked so heavy.

"Dirty money!" snarled Brother Hutton. "They stole it! Throw it in the privy."

Such a scramble of voices erupted, agreeing and disagreeing, that the chairman of the deacons commanded, "Hold your horses, folks. Let's count it."

Daddy, as church treasurer, stepped forward. He asked Brother Snider to witness his count. Silence prevailed while we stood still, watching intently.

At the end Daddy announced, "Forty-three dollars and seven cents."

I was stunned. In our Sunday collection plate we never got even a dollar altogether, not enough to buy literature for our Sunday School classes.

"We have no way to return it," said Miss Annie, trembling a little. "It's our responsibility now, to use for good."

"Amen," chimed in Miss Maude. "There's the children in the orphans' home."

"And don't forget our offering to missions," Miss Eula said.

"Oh, there's such a need everywhere," Miss Arlie added. "We can't throw it away."

And we didn't. We set to and parceled out the coins to the orphanage in Troy, to missions, and finally somebody gasped, "Eyeglasses for Brother Neale!" Daddy offered to drive him to the dime store in Tuscaloosa and help fit him with a pair of their best fifty-cent spectacles. Then those of us who taught Sunday School ordered pretty colored cards for our students to take home after each class. At the end of the semester they would have a collection to look through and recall what they had learned (we hoped).

And we still had enough coins for one of our most important traditions, the giving of bags of fruit and nuts to everyone who attended the Christmas Eve service. People who never came to church at any other time of year would walk from miles around for this treat.

We never learned where those hooded men came from or who they were or why they chose us, and they never came back. But we lost Brother Hutton. He stormed out, declaring he would not be part of a church that used dirty money. The rest of us worked on cleaning up that money by how we spent it.

17

Depression Wedding

As I grew older and bigger I could do more of the outside chores. I enjoyed working with the animals. I watered and fed the calves and curried them and looked after their hooves. Jack went with me to find succulent grass to cut for the milk cow. I cleaned the manure from the stalls and hauled it in the wheelbarrow to spread on the garden. Jack went with me to the neighbor's for her kitchen garbage to mix with ours and slop the pigs. I split wood and kindling for the cookstove and cleaned the chicken house. Francys, Jane, and Mary Alice looked after the kitchen jobs and the rest of the house.

Sometimes though I had to take a turn in the kitchen, always on a Sunday, the hardest day. That was because my sisters invited their friends from Little Hurricane Baptist for midday dinner, and Mama and Daddy, who attended Big Hurricane Baptist, brought home with them churchgoers who would find it too hard to walk to their homes and then return for the nighttime service.

"We can't leave them at the church alone and hungry," Mama said. Usually the preacher came with them. I bit my tongue not to complain, remembering what I'd learned in Sunday School: "God loveth a cheerful giver." I had to give my work cheerfully and do a good job of it.

One cloudy Sunday afternoon in January 1937 I had just finished washing what seemed like a mountain of dishes and was hanging the dishpan on a nail behind the stove when Mary Alice rushed in.

"Guess what! LeeOla and James are at the front door. They want the preacher to marry them!"

"Sure 'nuff?" I said, surprised. In these hard times people didn't often get married. They couldn't afford to.

"Come on! Grace and Verna are here too and their little brother."

I looked down at my work outfit—a ragged brown sweater over a dirty blue skirt and old tennis shoes with holes punched out by my big toes.

"I look too awful."

"You can sit in the back," she said. "Nobody'll notice."

I had never been to a wedding. I couldn't miss this one, so I followed Mary Alice into the dining room and sat down on a stool behind her. Alma and Trevena, who had helped dirty all those dishes I'd just washed, were squeezed into a chair beside her.

The double doors opening into the living room gave me a good view of Grace and her little brother sitting together in a chair near the front windows, her sister Verna to one side near the heater, and Mama and Daddy between the dining room and living room.

In the middle of the living room under the chandelier stood James and LeeOla facing the preacher who was studying the marriage license. LeeOla looked pretty but anxious. She wore a gray jacket and skirt with a red satin blouse that set off her tanned skin and curled brown hair. I had not seen her since the end of our sixth-grade year when so many of my classmates quit school. She was a year older than me.

"I'm not sure I can remember all the service," Preacher Mayfield said with a nervous frown. He continued looking at the license. Finally he cleared his throat, jerked at his tie, and said, "Well, what I can remember will do, I think."

He started out, his voice strong. "Dearly beloved, we are gathered together here in this place . . ." He faltered, blinking his eyes and wrestling mentally.

Everybody in the room sat still and quiet. The blue clock tick-ticking on the mantel under Grandmother's painting sounded loud and steady. I held my breath for fear the preacher would give up. In the suspended quiet I wondered how I'd like being married in such surroundings. Not that I didn't love the old house but everything was like me—worn and ragged. The flimsy cheesecloth curtains on the two big windows were trimmed with limp yellow ruffles. The chair Grace sat in had a broken rocker. Behind her the windowpane was missing, smashed when I threw a shoe at Buddy. Windowpanes cost half a week's wages, so Daddy had covered the hole with pasteboard to keep out the cold north wind. The small windows on each side of the fireplace were bare. The once-grand Victrola stood broken in the corner beside the antique table with the split marble top. The old scratched linoleum rug—

I was getting nail-biting nervous. So was the bride. She began whispering to the groom. Outside the clouds were heavy and dark but a sudden burst of sunshine seemed to jump-start the preacher. This time he persevered all the way through to the end when he said, "What God hath joined together let no man put asunder. I now pronounce you man and wife." After he prayed God's blessing on the couple, everybody crowded around them shaking hands and wishing them happiness. I was careful to hover in the background.

"The groom ought to kiss the bride," Daddy said. LeeOla blushed and James turned away to pay the preacher.

I thought of Mama's delicious golden pound cake left from dinner. "How about cake and cold buttermilk?" I suggested.

But they were in a hurry to leave. The preacher saw to the proper signing of the license while James lamented how expensive it had been. Brother Mayfield said, "You're paying for the governor's limousine."

All of us followed them to the porch to see them off. Just as they went down the steps little brother Buddy, who had been napping in the front bedroom, came running out wearing his dirty union suit. As the car drove down the lane, we went back inside to talk events over and give thanks that Buddy hadn't come out in the middle of the ceremony. The preacher would have surely forgotten what little he remembered.

"They are brave," Mama said. "I believe this depression will never end."

"But it'll be the two of them together," Daddy said. "They'll make it."

18

Uncle Joe and the King of England

ANY DAY THAT I OPENED the mailbox and found a letter from Uncle
Joe instantly became a Great Day. I recognized his clear, large writing and his stationery, which was an off-white that looked like linen,
with interesting foreign stamps pasted in the upper right-hand corner
of the envelope. I would grab it up to see where in the world he was
now. He worked for Waterman Steamship Company in Mobile and the
ships he sailed on went all about the world. This envelope now told
me he was on a ship named *Afoundria* and the postmark said London,
England. As usual it was addressed to Daddy. I felt it all over to see
if there might be enclosures—maybe a money order to help us buy
food or a picture of him in his first mate uniform. How could I wait
till Daddy came home from work tonight? Well, I *had* to! We never
opened each other's mail.

It turned out this letter was worth waiting for. Uncle Joe had seen
the old king of England, George V! That is, he saw his casket. More
than that, he saw the new king, Edward VIII, the king's family, and
royal people from all over the world.

It was January 1936 and cold. Uncle Joe had been standing on
that London street for six hours right behind a guard, waiting for the
king's funeral procession. Several people offered him a pound—five
dollars—for his place, but as he had stood there that long, nearly frozen, he thought he'd just stay. The crowd was so jam-packed that he
could hardly breathe. Finally, Edward and his brothers, walking behind the king's casket, came in sight. Uncle Joe said that none of the

royal ladies walked. They rode in carriages and all of them looked very solemn.

One Englishman nearby remarked loudly that all they needed now to be sitting pretty was to get a Yankee queen. The bystanders surrounding Uncle Joe nearly ran that man out because as the Prince of Wales, the new king had a close friendship with an American, Mrs. Simpson. This did not please most of the English people, Uncle Joe wrote.

Interesting as Joseph's letters were, they could not compare with his first visit with us in May 1937. I was sixteen, sitting on the front porch with the rest of the family and concerned because Daddy and Francys were late coming home. Dark had settled over Brookwood and we worried that they'd had an accident. Mrs. Hellums, a far neighbor, sat on the porch with us waiting for her daughter, Lois. She'd ridden to Tuscaloosa with Daddy that morning.

In the yard stood two brothers, the Alstons. They said they had come to talk business with Daddy and would wait for him. We wondered what that could be about, especially because the brothers smelled like the whiskey bottles Mary Alice and Teensy picked up along the road to sell to the bootlegger.

Around the curve from town came a car going slowly. We held our breaths, watching. As it approached our lane entrance, it slowed even more and turned in. It was a heavier car than our lightweight flivver, we could tell. Could it be somebody coming to tell us bad news? The Alstons started walking down the lane to meet the car which stopped even with them.

"Is this where Mr. Kilgore lives?" we heard a man say.

Both the brothers leaned in the window beside the driver and puffed their whiskey breaths in his face. "Sure 'nuff," one of them said. "We come up here to see him but he's late. Could be he's had a wreck—you know the curves in this road is bad to cause wrecks specially with old cars like his."

The strange car rolled backwards. I leaped up, afraid the unknown man was going to leave before we could find out who he was. The Alstons let go of the car and the guy drove round to the back of the house. Mama went to see who it was. In the car lights I saw that

Mama went to the front of the car as the man came around the back.

Mama said, "Here I am. I'm Mrs. Kilgore." Then, as they met, she said, "Law, it's Joe."

Jane, looking and listening from the kitchen window, yelled to us, "It's Uncle Joe!"

Mary Alice and I, peering around the corner of the porch, gasped. Vaguely I remembered a long time ago I said when Joey came I'd run out and hug his neck. Well, I didn't hug his neck but I was the first one to shake his hand. I don't remember how I got there, whether I jumped off the end of the porch or came around down the steps. He had a box of candy tucked under his arm, "something for the children."

Joseph, here! What we'd dreamed about, talked about, hoped for, but never really expected. As events turned out Daddy and Francys came home safely, the Alston brothers and Mrs. Hellums with her daughter disappeared, and we had an interesting time around the supper table. Francys told a bit about her day in classes at the university, Daddy mentioned that one of the ladies who rode to work with him had given him a stack of magazines for us, but mostly Uncle Joe listened. He wanted to hear family news. He and his younger brothers and sisters had grown up in the orphanage in Talladega after the death of their parents. Uncle Joe left the orphanage at sixteen, went to Mobile, and began working for the steamship company. The kind of life he led made it hard for him to keep in touch with relatives so he was glad for any news.

The first day his visit started off with a bang! While we were at school, he went to town and bought a floor model Silvertone radio from Sears and Roebuck, a beauty with a shining green eye when you turned it on. He installed it in the living room. It was the first thing I saw when I walked in from school. I stood transfixed in front of the magic box that would put me in touch with New York City and the whole rest of the world. It was better to me than all the candy and ice cream he could buy. Slowly I reached out and touched the shining mahogany case. A phrase of Latin I had learned from Daddy's old dictionary flashed into my mind: *mirabile dictu*—too wonderful to tell.

The next day, Uncle Joe came to pick me up at school to go to Tuscaloosa. Riding in his car was so quiet and comfortable, very different from our Model A Ford. At the end of our lane, Mama waited with Jane and Mary Alice and little Buddy. At the university, Francys hopped in. By then we were getting a little crowded in the car but none of us cared.

We walked around town window-shopping, one of our favorite things to do. Then he took us to see the movie *Wake Up and Live*. It was a musical with lots of action and noise. I loved Alice Faye and was very interested in seeing Walter Winchell, a famous gossip columnist. We came out of the theater humming "Never in a Million Years." I thought the movie was grand!

Afterward he treated us to delectable ice cream at Ward's Drug Store on the corner just across the street from the theater. When he paid our bill he showed us his billfold. It was stuffed an inch thick with money. He let us pass a hundred-dollar bill around the table, each of us taking turns holding it. We'd never even seen a twenty-dollar bill.

Then we went to Kress Dime Store just down the street where he bought a can opener and coffee cups—he had noticed that we had needed them having seen us drinking out of jars. He wanted to buy more candy but we thought better not to eat so much now. Besides, he bought so many other delicious things that I had to make room for them: ham, bacon, steak, canned salmon, sardines, soups, pork and beans, vanilla wafers, and moon pies. We ooohhed and ahhhed as we unpacked his grocery bags. In addition to all of that, almost every afternoon he took us for a drive to buy more ice cream at Mr. Martz's store, twelve one-cup packets of assorted flavors each time.

After supper on summer evenings, while smoking his corncob pipe, he liked to talk about his experiences. I listened intently because I too wanted to be a sailor. I longed to see the world.

He enjoyed observing the bird life, he said. One time, when his ship was five hundred miles from land, he noticed a large flock of little birds come aboard. They roosted there all night and flew away the next morning. One night when he was on watch, several hundred miles from land, a big owl lit on the mast and spread its wings. They were as long as Joseph's arms. It too spent the night. Once in the English Channel a carrier pigeon came aboard. It was exhausted and the ship was going farther and farther away from land toward America, so Joseph put it in a cage, brought it to Mobile, and cared for it until the next trip his ship made to England. He put a note of explanation in the pigeon's message tube and released the bird in the English Channel. No reply ever came so we couldn't know the end of this story.

Sometimes his ship picked up a cargo of turtles in Key West, Florida, bound for New York City, where the restaurants made turtle soup out of them. The turtles traveled down below in the ship's hold.

"They're half as big as your living room. We turn them on their backs so they're helpless, and we don't give them food or water," he said. "They moan all night and all day in such a pitiful way, lamenting. I'm glad to get them unloaded in New York Harbor."

When his ship was anchored in the port of Hamburg, Germany, he said, their second mate recognized the German hired to guard their ship as a man he had captured during the 1918 war. The two of them sat out on deck and talked and laughed. The man had learned English while in the American prison so they had no trouble communicating.

The ships Uncle Joe sailed on were freighters but a few of them carried several passengers. He said he enjoyed them, especially Vina Barrett, a romance writer for *Sweetheart Magazine*. She told Joseph she fell in love with a football hero, a very handsome man with the prettiest long eyelashes. But after they married she found out they couldn't live on long eyelashes.

Most of all we enjoyed hearing again about his encounter with the royalty of the world. That was history!

The day came when Uncle Joe had to leave. How we missed him! But as Mama said, "You kids can't live such a rich life too long or you'll get sick." And I did get sick. He left behind his corncob pipe and I smoked it while writing the highlights of his visit in my diary. Before I'd covered the happenings of his first day, the world around me began shaking and trembling, my insides turned queasy, and I upchucked some of that rich life I'd been living.

19

Virgie's Grandmother

VIRGIE'S GRANDMOTHER, ADELIA SMITH, WAS a fixture in our community life. It seemed to me that she stayed busy doing good from sunrise to sundown. She sewed cushions for our church pews and attended every service to make sure the church survived the bleak days of the Depression. Every Thanksgiving, she supervised our church's contributions to the railroad car of food bound for the orphans' home. She oversaw the sprawling Smith house, the orchard, the field between their house and ours, and the livestock. She made sure that those elderly folks who lived alone always had food to eat. I did not see how we could get along without her, but when Jane told me the news in school that day in May 1937 I realized we'd have to.

"Mrs. Smith is dead," Jane said. I stared at her, disbelieving. I had heard Mrs. Smith was sick but death never entered my thoughts.

"She died earlier this morning," she continued. "Carrie Lee, a neighbor, and the nurse were bathing her. Mrs. Smith asked for a cup of coffee. The nurse hurried to the kitchen to make the coffee while Carrie Lee adjusted Mrs. Smith in bed so she could drink it comfortable. Mrs. Smith suddenly clutched Carrie Lee's hand, gasped, 'My children,' and died."

While I struggled to understand this, Jane added, "The nurse tried to restore her with shots in her arms but they did no good. Mr. Smith was sitting on the porch in his rocker when she died at eleven o'clock. He's still sitting there, not moving or speaking."

After supper that night, taking an armload of flowers, I went with

Mama over the stile and across the field to sit up with Mrs. Smith. She was laid out in her front room and looked beautiful—white hair, white dress, and white-lined casket. Flowers surrounded her. Mama and I added ours to them. Standing there beside her coffin I inhaled the lovely mix of fragrances: magnolia blossoms, geraniums, begonias, all kinds and colors of daisies and lilies, dark-red star anise from the woods, and most fragrant of all, the white cape jasmines.

The few women there were all neighbors. I found a stack of magazines and chose a corner out of the way to look through them. The night crept along and I noticed the women sort of gave out of talk. I was comfortable in my corner with my reading and dozed off often. About midnight, Miss Alice said, "Why don't we just close all the doors and go home?"

Granny Bates, the oldest one there, said, "Never! Not while I'm alive!"

"No, sir!" Carrie Lee said. "When I'm the one in the coffin, y'all better not leave me alone till I'm in the ground."

"Well, if we leave her, there's nothing can hurt her," Mama said.

"Who started this custom of sitting up anyway?" Susie Mae demanded. But everybody stayed and Miss Alice made coffee to revive them.

When daylight came Joe, Mrs. Smith's grandson, brought in side meat from the smokehouse for breakfast. But Miss Alice, who was Mrs. Smith's daughter-in-law, put it away and went to the cool closet where the hams were kept. "All of you are company and she'd want you to have the best—ham," she said.

Mama sliced the ham and tended to cooking it. Virgie's mother made milk gravy and ham gravy. The others made coffee and biscuits, grits and scrambled eggs. Oh, it was all so delicious I overstuffed myself.

Mama and I were home in time for Daddy to get off to work and us children to go to school. The last period at school was canceled so everybody could go to the funeral at Big Hurricane Baptist. Praise for Mrs. Smith seemed to be all folks talked about.

But one day Mrs. Stevens came to our house to buy a nickel's worth of buttermilk. She lived on the hill above the big spring and had a houseful of half-grown children. She was brown from long hours working in the sun and thin from little food and hard work.

"I look at Miz Smith different," she said in her quavering voice. "My John would work hard all day for her and she'd pay him little or nothin'. That last time she paid him with a mess of what she called soup bones, but there was not a shred of meat on them bones at all. Nothin' to flavor soup. Tired as John was I made him take those bare bones back to her and demand that she pay him somethin' my hungry chirren could eat." She paused then added, "Miz Smith was like that more than once."

After she left I said to Mama, "Could what she said be true?"

"I'm sure it's true. Mrs. Stevens is an honest woman. But what we have to do is remember Mrs. Smith as we knew her firsthand," Mama said. "Remember how generous she was with fruit from her orchard, and the kind things she did. Remember when you and Mary Alice had no clothes to wear to school. She sent pretty blue sweaters for you all and cloth for me to make you skirts. And she paid your way to see your first movie, the only one you've seen. That's the Mrs. Smith we knew."

As I thought over what Mama said, I remembered other generous things Mrs. Smith had done for me, especially the Thanksgiving dinner where I had such a good time. The movie she paid my way to was Eddie Cantor in *Roman Scandals*, which I thought was hilarious. I had relived the experience by writing it down, and my teacher submitted what I wrote to a contest in the *Tuscaloosa News*. It won an honorable mention! Mrs. Smith got my name in the paper!

I didn't come to an understanding of how Mrs. Smith treated the Stevens family, but even then I knew, just from knowing myself, that we humans are all imperfect and have a need to forgive each other.

20

Granny Price's Birthday Celebration

LITTLE HURRICANE BAPTIST CHURCH INVITED everybody to an all-day singing with dinner on the grounds on a Monday in September 1937. The celebration was in honor of Granny Price who had just turned ninety-four. Usually I stayed home on these all-days, relaxing in solitude with Jack, our collie, and the cats, drawing pictures of our daily happenings in my book or writing in my diary, and "looking after the place." But Granny Price was historic. For her I was putting on a dress and shoes and going. Her husband, Grandpa Joseph Price, had been preacher for about a half century at Big Hurricane Baptist Church where I attended with Mama and Daddy. He was buried in our cemetery beside some of their children. His Civil War sword had been found hidden in the chimney when his old house within sight of Little Hurricane Baptist was dismantled. This celebration was too special to miss.

At midnight as soon as Sunday was over—Baptists don't work on the Sabbath—Mr. Jolly Jones started the barbecuing. It was an all-night job because he had to first mix up enough of his special sauce for a whole calf, a whole pig, and a whole goat.

At our house that Monday morning, we assembled the food we were taking and packed it in our Model A Ford which Daddy didn't need for his work that day.

"Probably all this will be eaten," Mama said, "so if you want any supper you'd better help yourself to two pieces of barbeque."

By the time we arrived at the plain white church, the parking lot was filled and crowds of people stood around under the trees talking. The tables, set up in the shade behind the church, were already loaded. There was hardly squeezing room for Mama's biscuits, potato salad topped with slices of boiled eggs sprinkled with paprika, her golden pound cake and her mocha cake, and the platter filled with tomatoes, cucumbers, homemade pickles, and tender green onions.

On the main table were stacks of barbecued beef, pork, and goat surrounded by loaves of light bread. How my mouth watered as I walked around the tables inventorying what was available and smelling all the good odors. Sweet potatoes in every form—in pies and turnovers, and by themselves candied or baked—and apples the same. I recognized Miz Hudson's white-frosted cake with black walnut nutmeats pressed along the sides and Olabelle's huckleberry cobbler. Turnip greens, green beans, peas, yellow squash, fried green tomatoes, fried eggplant—before I was ready, Brother Wooley rapped for quiet and said the blessing. But I knew just where all my favorites were located and it didn't take me long to serve myself a heaping plate.

During dinner I managed to hide some meat for my supper, some leavings from other peoples' plates for Jack's supper, and a big bone for his dessert. How I longed for my overalls with all those pockets, but I managed concealment in the ruffles of a hand-me-down dress from Pittsburgh.

After dinner nearly everybody assembled in the church where Granny Price in her bonnet, long gray dress, and high-top shoes sat in the alcove behind the pulpit looking kind of absent. She probably had her corncob pipe in her apron pocket and longed to take a smoke.

During the program that followed, folks took turns going up to shake hands and greet her. I sat near the back of the church watching and listening as a choir sang hymns, a singing-school teacher presented her pupils in several selections, and quartets even I had heard of sang revival songs from long ago. When Granny Price's head nodded, two of her great-grandsons made a packsaddle of their arms for her to sit on and carried her down the center aisle of the church.

Everybody leaped to their feet and bawled out the hymn "Where We'll Never Grow Old." We stayed standing till her car was out of sight. I was sure that she'd prefer a wagon pulled by a red mule.

With Granny Price gone I turned my attention to the audience. A whole lot was going on. All the windows were propped open with broomsticks and all the hand fans were going lickety-split so we were not uncomfortable. I saw my sisters sitting with their friends in different sections of the church and Mama up front with the ladies. A small gray mouse ran around searching under the benches. I sprinkled some crumbs from Jack's supper at my feet in case he came my way.

Those near the windows could keep check on what was happening inside and outside. Sometimes they carried on a conversation with a friend who was standing outside on the grounds. At one point Otis, seated not far from me, leaned out the window and hollered, "Hey, Fred, come on in." His mama slapped him on the head with her fan, and the singing went on without interruption.

Out of the way, at the front of the church, lay several babies on the floor, limp in sleep. Under them was spread an embroidered crazy quilt. I noticed that one of them was still enjoying his homemade sugar tit even though he seemed unconscious. Their mothers could keep an eye on them while taking part in the singing.

At the backbenches sat courting couples busy with pencils changing the titles in the hymnals into complete sentences. I had read some that had been changed at other singings and found them funny: "I'll Fly Away" *with you to Hollywood Cali.* "Beulah Land" *is where Beulah lives.* "Were You There" *when Emmet kissed Mary Kate?* "When the Roll Is Called Up Yonder" *Wilber will be off in the swamp gigging frogs.* Some of them, though, were too racy to call to mind.

Often a singer had to wet a dry throat with a drink from the dipper in the bucket of water that was kept on a small table by the side door. One of the men made everybody laugh when he pulled at his tie and said, "I got to loosen my choke rag so I can sing better."

No girl dared leave the church to join the boys standing around outside. If she had to go to the outhouse, she must take a girl with her and come back inside right away. But most girls suffered rather than admit they needed to relieve themselves.

About four-thirty people began drifting out to their cars and driving away after claiming their dishes from the dinner tables. Through the open windows I heard them calling goodbyes to one another. I kept an eye on Mama because we had to get home to take care of our animals and she had to milk our cow. Finally she did stand up, and nodding to those around her, she came down the aisle signaling for us to follow.

For supper that night all of us had barbeque but not with light bread. Enough of Mama's biscuits had been left and a few other odds and ends to complete our meal. The cats shared Jack's supper and he took his dessert bone off to eat in privacy. We all went to bed feeling satisfied we'd done a good job of moving Granny Price along toward her ninety-fifth birthday.

21

Mrs. Prude and Her Sons

IN THE SETTLEMENT AROUND BROOKWOOD School, our house was on a hill by itself. About a quarter mile away toward the school, Mr. Bill Prude lived in the back room of the closed cotton gin. Every morning, rain or shine, freezing or scorching hot, he hobbled along the Birmingham–Tuscaloosa highway, his waist-length gray beard stirred by traffic backlash, to our house to sit and talk to Mama.

But Mama was not happy about these visits. "I can't get my work done," she complained. "I clean up the kitchen from breakfast, making your school lunches, and getting you four off to school. Then I need to take care of the outside chores and do a little hoeing. When I come inside there's churning and fixing up the butter, and sweeping and everything else. It's your daddy he should be talking to."

But Daddy was away working on the extra board of the Frisco Railroad, trying to earn enough money to help our family of seven survive the Depression.

Unlike Mama, I delighted in Mr. Prude's visits. The Prudes were a storied family to me because of Daddy's tales about them. One of my greatest joys in the spring was riding in our topless Model T under a canopy of blooming mimosa trees as we approached the Prude place just outside Tuscaloosa. The trees on both sides of the highway were covered with feathery pink blossoms and the air was intensely sweet with their fragrance. I looked up into the trees arching over us, longing to clasp one of those blossoms in my hands. When we passed the driveway leading in to the big house, I could see that the mimosas continued right up to the portico with its white columns.

To think, my daddy had lived in that house! For four years when he was a boy! Built before the Civil War, the house was haunted, of course. Daddy had told us how he and his brother Davis lay awake late at night listening to the long-dead Mr. Prude tap-tap-tapping with his walking stick past their room on his way out the back hall door toward the cedar tree where the pot of money was buried.

That was the treasure that my daddy and his brother had dug for when they were boys. It had been meant for William Liberty Kilgore, our grandfather. He was orphaned by the Civil War and the elder Prudes took him in. William Liberty appreciated what they did for him and he tried to do everything he could to help them. When he grew up he got a job in a Cottondale store as a clerk. He was so dependable that he soon worked his way up to handling the finances of the store.

Every Saturday was payday for the cotton mill and other local businesses, and his job was to collect the money owed to the store from the workers before they spent their pay on new purchases. It was the busiest day and the most important day the store had.

Late one Friday night William Liberty was notified at his boardinghouse in Cottondale that Mr. Prude wanted to see him. William explained to the messenger that he couldn't walk the three miles to the Prude place in the dark and get back to the store by six the next day, when he had to start taking the customers' payments. He couldn't be late.

But the next morning, even before William Liberty was out of bed, the messenger appeared again. "You'd better come now. The old man is dying."

William was torn. He had never disobeyed his foster father before but the store depended on him.

"I'll come the very first minute I can," William promised desperately. And he did, almost running the three miles from Cottondale to the Prude place.

"But he was too late," Mr. Bill told Mama at the churn and me sitting at our kitchen table listening with both ears. "My pa died standing in that back room—I can see him now—one elbow on the mantel, looking out the window toward that big cedar tree."

Bill Prude went on talking. "'There's something I want William Liberty to have,' Pa said at the last. 'Some papers and—ah—things.' But he dropped in his tracks standing there and could never utter another word before death claimed him." Mr. Bill paused to gather his thoughts. "There was always bad feelings between Brother Oscar and me," he said. "And Brother Oscar especially hated William Liberty. He wouldn't stand to hear a good word about him. And when William Liberty married and had a son—your pa," he nodded at me, "and named him William for me and Oscar for my brother—that sure tumped over the wagon with my brother. But our ma was as plumb tickled as our pa. Now about then Brother Oscar was sheriff of the county. He sent drovers out to William Liberty's farm to foreclose on his herd of cattle and drive them away. William had to go to court to get his cattle back."

As the two Prude brothers aged, their jealousy and hatred of one another increased, according to Mr. Bill. Their mother was much grieved by the bad feeling between her sons. Mr. Bill told us that when his mother became seriously ill she sent for them. The sons did not speak to each other but stood on opposite sides of their mother's bed. The family's elderly Black nurse, Rueanna, stood at the head of the bed listening and watching.

"Boys," Mrs. Prude said so low and trembly her sons leaned over to hear. "I know that you two can't get along. I've prayed about you, but I'm afraid that after I'm gone you are going to kill each other."

Oscar and Bill didn't deny it.

"I love you both. I want you to lay your right hands on my heart here, and promise me that after I'm dead you won't do harm to one another."

The sons made no move. Their mother, far gone as she was, made an effort and caught each of their hands and placed them on her heart. Then she placed her hand on top of theirs.

"Now boys," she whispered, "promise 'In Mama's name, dear Lord, I will never hurt my brother.'"

The two stood like stone posts.

The old lady coughed. "Listen close, my sons. If I die without your promise I will never rest. I will be an ever-present revenant in your lives. Guarding you from each other." She coughed again and her breathing became more like pants.

Bill said softly, "Mama, I promise."

Rueanna, the only person not scared of Oscar, seized his ear and twisted. "Answer your mama. Now!" And she twisted harder. But it was too late. Mrs. Prude was dead and Oscar hadn't promised. He shoved the nurse aside, saying to Bill, "Just you wait till the will's read," and he strode from the room rubbing his ear.

Oscar inherited everything but Bill said the will was a fake. "If the true will could have been found I wouldn't be a penniless old man living in the back of a cotton gin today," he said to Mama and me.

Of course he wasn't in want. Alice Prude Smith, his daughter, kept his big room clean and comfortable. I had seen with envy all the magazines and books he had available and Miss Alice's cook brought his meals to him. I saw nothing wrong in his setup. I would have changed places with him in a flash, bookless and magazineless as I was, and sometimes even low on food.

"Oscar Prude died a rich, rich man," Rueanna told me at the Box Springs Community Store when I was visiting my teacher Mrs. Wilson who owned the store. "But he never had a minute's peace to enjoy it. He was scared to death. He heard voices calling him. Away in the night he heard pounding on the front door. He saw visions of angels and devils. All the poor folks he'd cheated, those he'd stolen from, the ones he'd jailed unrightly—haunted him. Most of all, his mama came back just like she said she would. Yes, he was rich, rich, but he paid for it."

"He must have had some good in him," I reminded Rueanna. "His monument in old Evergreen graveyard says 'to the memory of precious Papa.'"

Rueanna closed her eyes for a long two moments of silence. I wondered what pictures of the past she was seeing. Then she opened her eyes and said sincerely, "I'm glad he was precious to somebody."

22

Belle

I WAS ALWAYS GLAD TO hear that Belle was back. Every fall, as soon as cold weather took over, she came from Mississippi and stayed till summer warmth moved in. I'd see her in the mornings when I went for the table scraps that the Madaris family saved to help feed our pigs. She'd be sitting in a rocking chair on her son's porch, wearing her long hair neatly balled on top of her head, a clean dress down to her ankles, and a smile on her face. She looked like last year's walnut with the hull beaten off—small, shriveled, and black. Belle's son worked in Mr. Madaris's sawmill and his wife, Leanna, cooked for the Madaris family. Their shotgun house stood beside the Madarises' house.

"Hey, Belle," I hollered from the gate. "It's time you came back. How you been?"

"Good enough, I reckon," she answered. "I'm glad to be here where I can't hear them hungry cows bellerin' for food."

"Are things bad in the Delta?" I asked.

"Real bad. Ain't no feed for the animals and mighty little for the folks. Not been any rain for months."

After a bit more talk, I moved on with a lighter step to the Madarises' kitchen. Having Belle to look forward to on the slop run made me forget my fear that some member of my class would pass on the road and see me toting slop and wearing my ragged work outfit.

As usual, every morning the numerous Madaris family was in chaos. Mr. Madaris came out the door as I tried to go in. He was hurrying with a spatula in his hand to shout at several of his boys in the garden who were chasing chickens.

"Shoo them," he hollered. "Chunk rocks! Don't let 'em eat up the beans." He whirled and rushed back into the kitchen to turn over the steak that was frying in a huge iron skillet.

How mouth-watering good it smelled! I took a glance at it—deep tan and crusty—before exchanging my clean bucket for the full bucket behind the stove. Leanna was at the corner shelves searching for something.

"Ohhh, gosh," she said, sighing as she turned back to the stove and opened the oven door. "And now I done burned the biscuits!"

Mr. Madaris was jabbering at her in his excitable way. Leanna had to ask him to repeat himself over half the time, on account of how fast he talked.

"Open another jar of that plum jam," I understood him to say. "And get out the butter."

"Huh? What you say?" Leanna already knew all this. She'd been doing it for years.

"Set that dozen eggs to boiling too," he added as he turned steaks.

I paid him no mind. It was the food that got my attention every morning.

In the yard again I saw that the boys were still chasing chickens. Now it was a game. When they got two of them out of the garden, three went in. As soon as Mr. Madaris appeared again yelling directions, the boys turned serious.

Some mornings the porch rocking chair was vacant, and I'd find Belle in the kitchen along with Leanna and Mrs. Madaris's stepmother.

"I made the biscuits," Belle told me with a grin. "Lookee here." She lowered the oven door. There were two pans full of the biggest biscuits I'd ever seen—saucer-sized. They had puffed up and out, and were browning most beautifully.

"Whee!" I said in admiration.

"Nobody don't need two o' my biscuits," she said with satisfaction.

"They must be delicious," I said. "I never see one of them in the slop bucket."

She laughed. "That's sure the truth."

In one of our porch talks Belle lamented about young folks today. "They got their minds on all kinds of shenanigans they oughtn't to be doing—dancing and movies and such. They should be attending a gentle concert or a singing."

I didn't point out to her that none of us had concerts, gentle or otherwise, that we could attend. And I had coveted movies ever since Virgie's grandmother took me to see Eddie Cantor. But when I told her about my history teacher she cackled.

"He's real tall," I said. "Got a big nose and he looks down it at us kids. He knows French and Latin." And I spoke some of his languages, distorted by my Southern accent. "Ago, Amee, Tay. Billay doo. Cher shay la famme," I said. "Veni, vedee, vechee."

Belle was enchanted. After that, sometimes she'd greet me with one of his phrases further distorted by her Delta drawl.

She laughed the heartiest when I told her about a test that Teacher gave us. One of the questions was, "Who is the Head of the Church?"

"We all knew the answer, all of us Baptists and Holy Rollers," I told her. "God, of course."

Belle nodded vigorously.

"Next day when Teacher handed back our papers, he was in a mighty rage," I said. "He gave us to understand that the pope is the head of the church. We had heard of the pope but he didn't have anything to do with us. We all knew God and most of us said our prayers to Him every night. Teacher spent the whole class period preaching about the pope being the head of the church. He was still mad the next day. And you know what?" Belle shook her head in suspense. "Every test after that the first question on it was, 'Who is the Head of the Church?'"

"What did you chillun do?" she breathed.

"We wrote in that blank 'The Pope.' We must have had a hundred tests in history the rest of the year and that was always one of the questions. And we always wrote in 'The Pope.' We knew it wasn't true but it pleased Teacher and at the end of the year we all passed!"

That tickled her most of all. "Y'all won," she said, grinning.

Sometimes tiny Belle complained about herself. "I ain't nothin' but a big old blunderbuss. After dinner I was helping clear the table when there was kinfolks visiting. I was pouring out the ice tea glasses into your slop bucket. In a hurry, I grabbed up the glass full of soggum syrup, and poured it in too. What a scandal! I couldn't get it back so there was nothin' to do but refill the syrup glass."

"You couldn't help it," I comforted her. "Soggum syrup looks just like tea."

"That don't excuse me none," she said.

"Well, no matter what you say, you're not a blunderbuss. We've got a blunderbuss behind our kitchen door, and my daddy says if anybody pulls the trigger, it'll explode. You not goin' to explode, are you?"

"I just might. I don't even have walking around sense."

I laughed. "Anyway, you gave our pigs a big treat, thank you."

"I didn't mean to do it so no thanks to me," she said.

During one of the tent meetings, Belle rode there with Mrs. Madaris. They parked out in the dark where they had a good view of the goings-on. It was one of those "forgiving" nights when there was lots of hugging and crying and praying. Miss Linnie, at the altar, rassled aloud with a call from God that she didn't want to accept.

"You want me to start a home for homeless boys, Honored Lord. You see all the abandoned boys roaming hither and yonder. I see them too and my heart's torn for the little lost lambs. But, Lord, don't you see too that I have no money to build such a place? I've got no land to build anything on, and no know-how about building, and I don't know flugins about boys. What would I feed a houseful of boys? How could I clothe them? Sir, please don't ask it of me. I'm not the one. No, no, not me. I'm too old and tired . . ." Everybody was in the prayer with her because we knew she was telling the Lord the truth but the Lord didn't back down. Miss Linnie got up from her knees wiping the tears from her face. "The Lord won't relent," she said. "He stands firm."

The next morning when I went into the Madaris kitchen Belle examined my face. "Did you cry your eyes out over that Miss Linnie? That little woman sure can pray. But she's wastin' her time buckin' God. He don't take no for an answer."

Belle still hadn't left for the Delta in June 1937 when rabies vaccination time came. I was glad because I wanted her to see me dressed up for once and this was a social occasion. All sorts of people attended vaccination day, bringing their dogs or just coming to visit. At our house we bathed Jack and brushed his long collie coat. I borrowed my sister's shoes and put on a purple taffeta dress sent from the relatives in Pittsburgh. We searched the house to scrape together the fifty cents to pay for the vaccination, then Mama and I started walking to the store with Jack prancing at the end of his rope.

Belle was on her porch. Mrs. Madaris's stepmother stood at the gate talking to her. They hushed and looked at us.

Belle shaded her eyes. "Is that my slop girl?" she marveled. "Ain't she pretty? And just look at her highfalutin dog. Where you going?"

I explained and promised to tell her all about it tomorrow.

Belle was still marveling. "That's my slop girl," she told the step-mother. "She's too pretty to tote slop, ain't she?"

I laughed. "There aren't many people who aren't too pretty to tote slop."

"That ain't so," she rejoined with spirit. "You're the prettiest one."

With a wave, Mama, Jack, and I went on our way. Under a big tree at Mr. Martz's store I saw pickups, mule-drawn wagons, oxcarts, and rattletraps parked every which way. Ninety-five dogs—I counted them—and even more people crowded around the veterinarian and his chopping block. I saw right away that Jack was the biggest, pretti-est, and oldest dog there. He knew it too and was itching to show off. He finally challenged the wrong dog, one that had a gang of friends to come to his aid. I had to wade into the melee to save him.

When the veterinarian's assistant lifted Jack to the chopping block for his shot, the vet frowned at me. "Getting in the middle of a dog fight is not a wise thing to do, little lady. It's a good way to get that pur-ple dress torn into shreds."

I well knew that but where our faithful Jack was concerned I didn't care. The vet sent into the store for four Buffalo Rock ginger ales, one for him, one for his helper, one for Mama, and one for me. It was the first one I'd ever tasted and I was delighted. It chilled and stung my insides as it went down. I turned that bottle up over and over again to drain the last drop. I read every word printed on the glass sides, trying to hold on to the pleasure.

I was interested to look over the different kinds of dogs and their owners. Even the most scroungy dog seemed to be valued by his human. The exception was Virgie's uncle John surrounded by his gang of thin, hungry-looking fox-hunting hounds. Mr. Givens kept his redbone hound apart while he chatted with Mr. Raines, who didn't have a dog but always came for the visiting. Bertha's daddy and Archie kept their dogs together, and Otis had a square-jawed, pointy-eared young dog like I'd never seen before.

"He's a pit bull, a fighter," Otis said. "I'm getting him ready for that varmint when it comes back."

"He's got to grow a whole lot before he's ready for the Horror," I said.

"He's young but he'll grow fast 'cause I'm feeding him good. I don't let anybody pet him. I want him to be fierce."

I looked around. "I don't see Willett."

"Didn't you hear?" Otis said. "His dog got run over. By a Dixie Coach bus. Mashed her flat."

Willett and I didn't get along but I was sorry about his dog. She was the only thing Willett loved. He never looked very clean himself but he'd kept her bathed and groomed. She was a little beauty.

I kept watching the road toward the old Lawrence place and finally I saw Mr. Criss and his dog Bill coming. Jack and I walked to meet them. Bill was well primped for this day. He and Jack were both handsome and pepped up but they didn't take to each other.

"We'd best separate them," Mr. Criss said.

Several people we knew from the Quarters stood with their dogs straining at their ropes. There was Aunt Susie, the baby-birther and fortune-teller, Aunt Janie and Mr. Will with their oxcart, and Julia, who told Mama, "I oughta be home right now chopping my cotton."

"What're your dogs' names?" I asked Julia. Her answer tickled me and I filed it away carefully so I could tell Belle the next day.

The next morning Belle met me at the gate and enjoyed every word of my story. When I came to the part about Julia's dogs, I said, "She had three. One was named Tripod—that one had three legs—another was Beulah, and you'll never guess what her third dog was named. She was little and black and a know-it-all."

"Ring," Belle guessed.

"No. She was solid black."

"Rattler."

"She wasn't pied. She was solid black."

"King."

"She was a girl dog."

"Queenie."

"Nope. Remember, she's a know-it-all like me."

"Give up," Belle said.

"What kinda name could she have but Belle?"

We laughed so hard that we had to hold on to each other to keep from falling down.

Belle and I didn't suspect that our days together were numbered. By 1939 Mr. Madaris had cut all the timber available in our area and he had to move his sawmill to another part of Alabama. The last time I saw Belle she was in the porch rocker, neat and sparkly, ready for the day.

"Well, how are you today?" I called from the gate.

She called back, "Tolerable well, I reckon, for an old soul 'bout to die."

I had never thought of her dying. She seemed indestructible. Her words shocked me into a shout of laughter. And she was so surprised at my laugh that she gave me one of her biggest grins.

As it turned out, what happened was a lot like when someone died. Belle's son, foreman of the sawmill, moved with it, taking Leanna and Belle with him. Our family mourned their going.

"Mrs. Madaris was the best neighbor we ever had," Mama said. We remembered when Buddy got choked on a whole peach pickle. He was turning blue when Mrs. Madaris came to help. After we had him breathing again, she said, "We had an ole preacher one time who said, 'There oughtn't to be no Hell for any woman who raises a bunch of young'uns.'"

"Amen, amen!" I had said, still shaking from fright.

And sometimes when we had nothing to eat in the house, one of us would run down to the Madaris house and borrow a can of salmon.

Mama made delicious croquettes for us when we hadn't expected to have anything.

Once we had an important letter to mail, but a search of our house did not turn up the three cents we needed for postage. I hurried to the back of the field where Sid was hoeing. His pockets were empty. We *had* to mail the letter. The mailman was almost due. Jane ran to Mrs. Madaris's and borrowed the three cents, and the letter got mailed.

Even our pigs missed the Madaris family.

And I missed Belle most of all.

23

Teensy's Family

TEENSY GREEN STAYED AT OUR house more than she stayed at her own. After five days or so Mama would say to her, "Teensy, you need to let your mother know that you're all right." She'd disappear for a day and a night then reappear at our door. Other times Mrs. Green, frail as a haint, walked the two miles down the road to our house to see about Teensy. Mama took time out from her many chores to visit with Mrs. Green, offering her a glass of milk and inviting her to lie down awhile. She always refused. For one thing, she preferred snuff to any food you could name. The whole family, except for Teensy, dipped.

Often in summer our long table was filled with eaters—preachers, my sisters' friends, and always Teensy. One dinner time when Mama set Grandmother's blue pitcher filled with tea on the table, Teensy stared at the windmill on it and the Dutch boy and girl kissing. Suddenly she broke out laughing. "Look at them," she said. "They're rubbing noses." We laughed, realizing for the first time that she didn't know what kissing was.

Teensy's father, Elec, was deaf as a cedar post but he made good crops every year—beautiful peaches, excellent watermelons and corn, and prolific peas, all due to the hard work of Teensy's teenage brothers, Thomas and William. Mr. Green sold the produce from a roadside stand in front of their house. In his overall pocket he kept a big roll of bills, but his family had little benefit from the money because Mr. Green's "friends" got him drunk and stole it.

One late summer we picked peas for Mr. Green on halves: our

family would get half of all the peas we picked, and Mr. Green would get the other half. What a hot job it was, us thirsty, hungry barefooted young'uns dragging our tow sacks full of peas through ants, stinging nettle, and worse, bull nettle. But we knew if we wanted food in the winter, we had to pick peas now. Mr. Green didn't pick, Mrs. Green wasn't able, and Francys and Jane stayed home with Buddy, but the rest of us pitched in—my parents, Mary Alice, me, Thomas, William, and Teensy. We owed many tasty winter meals to Mr. Green's generosity.

After a violent storm that lasted most of the night, we were all sleeping late on a Saturday morning when we heard a loud knocking on the back door and a man's voice shouting. "Hello! Hello!"

Only Daddy stirred. He went to the door in his nightshirt to find Mr. Hambright, who lived in a two-room house back of us. Snug under the covers as I was I couldn't hear what went on, but Daddy came away from the door saying, "What a way to start the day—waking up the whole house just to ask if he can catch a ride to town with me." Mama said something I didn't understand, and Daddy added, "He'll be back after we have breakfast."

Before Daddy got settled in bed again we heard another holler. "Howdy, Mr. Kilgore." Teensy's daddy.

"No peace for the weary," Daddy groaned. "Elec! What are you doing running around this time of day?" He said it just natural so Mr. Green didn't hear him.

Mr. Green said, "I didn't see no smoke coming out of the kitchen chimney so I warn't going to wake you up. But then that Hambright fellow come and put in his bid to go to town. You got room for me?"

"I reckon. Come on in," Daddy shouted. "Have a seat while I get some clothes on."

Daddy, grumbling every step of the way, left Mr. Green in the living room. By this time Mama was up and on her way to the kitchen and Mary Alice was up trying to find her shoes.

"Didn't you leave them in the living room?" Jane asked.

So Mary Alice went into the living room where Mr. Green ensnared her with an involved story about a mousetrap. Out of politeness she stayed, putting on her shoes while listening.

When he paused she thought he'd finished so she left. He followed her down the hall to the kitchen still telling his mousetrap story. Mama interrupted to invite him to sit down and have a cup of coffee. While Mama continued with breakfast, frying bacon now, the two of them discussed the Hambrights. Mr. Green naturally talked loud and Mama had to holler to make him hear her so I was sure the Hambrights heard every word they said. I lay in bed laughing till my stomach hurt. When Mama called us to breakfast she invited Mr. Green to the table too. Teensy had eaten with us hundreds of times but this was the first time for one of her parents.

As Mary Alice had moved on up into high school and Teensy continued to stay out of school, they no longer saw each other. I dared not ask Mr. Green what had happened to Buck and Buddy, the girls' trained mounts. I knew the fate for calves on a farm when they grew into beef size.

In October 1938 Mrs. Green sent Teensy's brother Thomas to tell Mama that she was sick. The boy was so shy he could hardly get the words out past his lip full of snuff. "Mama said would you—uh—ask the preacher to come to see her." He paused, struggling. "She's a-thinking she won't get well. She—she wants to join the church."

Mama told the preacher and he did get there in time as Mrs. Green hung on to life till March 1939. During that while, Mama sometimes prepared a tray for her, making a fire in the wood stove, scraping together food to appeal to a sick person, then walking two miles carrying it. But near the end Mrs. Green was almost too weak to eat anything.

Early on the morning of March 29, Mr. Burrage, a far neighbor of the Greens, appeared at our back door to say that Mrs. Green had died and there was nobody at the house with Teensy and her two brothers, Thomas and William. Mama went, even though rain was pouring down.

Above the noise of the rain on the tin roof, Teensy told Mama that just before her mother died she called her husband over to her bed and said, "Mister Green, are you going home with me?"

"Pa's so deaf he couldn't understand what she was saying," Teensy added.

Next day Mama gathered a large bouquet of lilacs, roses, and crepe myrtle to take for the burial.

The rest of the family continued living in the house however they could. As it was spring, plowing and planting had to continue. A month after Mrs. Green died, Mr. Green dreamed about her. She stood by his bed wearing a red dress. Next day he looked up "red" in the dream book he kept tucked behind the wall clock.

"It says if you dream about red there's gonna be a happening that'll make blood.'" Teensy's father told her. "Blood. I ain't staying in this house another minute."

"Where'll you go?" she asked.

"Tom's, I reckon. At Klondike."

And off he went to stay with his brother about two miles along the highway. Two days later when Mr. Green came walking back to check up on things, a man he knew pulled his pickup off on the opposite side of the road and hailed him. Mr. Green started across the road to talk to him, not looking first and not hearing the blaring horn or squealing brakes of an oncoming truck trying to avoid him. Nothing could save him though the truck wrecked in the ditch trying to.

"Yeah, there was red everywhere, blood and more blood," Teensy said when she came to our house to ask for funeral flowers. Mama had a big bouquet ready to take herself.

Teensy was wearing a dress, the first I'd ever seen her in, and looked grown-up. Pretty—brown eyes, lively brown hair, clear skin, and amazingly good teeth considering all the sweets she and Mary Alice had bought with their business profits.

"I'm not Teensy anymore," she told Mama. "I go by my real name now. Gladys."

We trusted that Mr. Green's brothers would help his orphaned children. We couldn't, with Daddy working away from home so much and our days crowded with our work and caring for our farm.

24

Uncle Nat Helps Raise a Submarine

IN THE SUMMER OF 1937 Uncle Nathaniel came to visit us driving what I called a good-looking car. I didn't know what kind of car. I just knew it was long and shiny. He still lived in New York but Agnes was not with him this time as they had divorced. We regretted that. We thought Agnes was unusual but we liked her.

The youngest of Daddy's brothers, Nathaniel had lived in the orphanage at Talladega from about age four until he ran away to join the Navy at age sixteen. He and Daddy didn't have many memories to share, but he did recall hearing about the buzzard-trapping adventure Daddy and Uncle Davis had at the Prude place. Mostly he talked about life in New York, but one night after supper when we were all gathered on the front porch, he mentioned that because of his looks—a baby face with a dimpled chin—he had a hard time when he first joined the Navy.

"Those tough sailors never let up teasing me. I had to learn to be as rough as they were," he said. "I had so many fights the Navy threatened to assign me to the *Pittsburgh*, the ship with the roughest reputation in the whole Navy."

But he stayed put where he was and his ship was sent on a goodwill tour of Europe. While there they heard about the sinking of the submarine *S-51* in September 1925 off the east coast of the United States near Block Island. Several ships had tried unsuccessfully to raise the submarine. In May 1926 Uncle Nat's ship was ordered home and assigned that job.

"A whistling buoy marked the place where the sub was rammed," Uncle Nat told us. "It was sure eerie hearing that buoy. The rougher the weather got, the louder the buoy moaned. Whooooooooooo." His imitation of the wailing buoy rolled down our quiet hill and into the woods. It made our dog Jack raise his head and prick up his ears.

Every sailor aboard Nat's ship vowed not to shave until they succeeded in bringing up the sub.

"We were a funny-looking bunch," he said. "Some beards were long and black, some bushy red, and a few curly blond. I was too young to grow a beard, so I grew long sideburns. We laughed to see our pictures in the newspapers and in the newsreels when we went to the picture show."

Nat's crew succeeded in raising the *S-51* in July 1926. When the sub was opened, doctors wearing white gloves were lowered inside and stretchers sent down to bring up the bodies. There had been only one Black crew member aboard the *S-51*, but Uncle Nat was on deck where the bodies were laid out and saw the wind blow the sheets off of them. They had all turned black.

"The bodies fell apart and the odor made me sick. You didn't go on deck unless you had to. Only forty fellows were found," he said. "Six were never accounted for. Three managed to escape but the radio antennae caught one of them and dragged him down. The other two were exempted from ever going to sea again. But one of those guys refused the exemption. He said, 'Naw, that didn't scare me,' and was assigned to another ship. Don't you know, two months later an explosion aboard that ship killed him, nobody else."

When their work of three months was done, Uncle Nat and his shipmates went ashore at Newport to celebrate. They ended up in jail charged with drunkenness, disorderly conduct, resisting arrest, breaking windows out of a taxicab (they hadn't been near a taxi, Uncle Nat claimed), and a page full of other crimes.

The judge said, "Guilty or not guilty?"

The sailors who pleaded guilty paid a fine and went free to rejoin their ship. Uncle Nat and a buddy pleaded not guilty.

The judge said to them, "Eight weeks or fifty dollars." They didn't have fifty dollars so they were taken back to jail and locked up. Uncle

Nat watched through the cell bars as his ship steamed out of the harbor blowing her whistle.

He rethought his position. As this was a new courthouse, lots of money was needed to pay for it. He might get a better deal from the judge if he pleaded guilty and paid the fine. He called the guard and told him he wanted to change his plea.

The judge sent for him. "Guilty or not guilty?" he asked.

Uncle Nat said, "Guilty."

The judge said, "Ten dollars and costs."

Nat paid twelve dollars and hitchhiked after his ship. Because he was five days over his leave, he expected to be sentenced to the brig for a stretch. However, all the captain said was, "We'll wait and see when the other guy gets back." But when that last sailor rejoined the crew nothing was ever said about punishment.

We sat silent for a while after Uncle Nat's New York accent faded into the night. Then Daddy said, "That seems fair enough after what you all had been through."

Other family members who expressed themselves agreed. I said nothing, but after I went to bed, I couldn't get to sleep thinking of those sailors stuck under water for so long. Of how much hard work went into trying to bring up the submarine. And how odd those sailors, who finally raised it, must have looked as they went about their work. However, I decided that no matter how much I longed to see the world, I would never try to do it Uncle Nathaniel's way by joining the Navy. It was just as well I made this decision for later I realized that the Navy of that time did not accept women.

25

Aileen Discovers Football

MY SISTERS AND I DIDN'T go to football games at school because we never had the dime for admission. Football had no part in my life. But I woke up in a hurry one Saturday night in 1937 when I was at a meeting at the University of Alabama. I learned about the Crimson Tide! The meeting was to encourage country children to stay in school and amount to something. I was sitting with Virgie and several other Brookwooders in Morgan Hall waiting for the meeting to begin when we saw a young man come in at the back and walk down the aisle past us.

"Ooooh, did you see HIM?" Virgie whispered. We were all seeing him—handsome, composed, looking not left or right. We had seen his picture in the paper so often we knew him instantly. Bubba Nesbit, captain of the Crimson Tide!

"Let's get his autograph!" Nell breathed.

"Would you dare?" I asked.

"Sure. Come on, y'all."

And four of us followed Virgie down the aisle to where he sat alone in the front row. He was even handsomer up close. He smiled and stood up when Virgie made our request.

"Surely. I'll be glad to," he said. I'd never seen such beautiful white teeth. He signed our song sheets, looking us in the eyes as he handed them back.

"Thank you," we chorused and floated back to our seats, restraining our thrilled giggles until we were out of his hearing, we hoped.

He spoke last on the program and his subject was clean living. Lost in a fog of admiration, we heard little of what he said. I marveled at his poise. He spoke without notes and was so calm before this auditorium full of gawky teenagers.

When he sat down I thought the applause would never stop. We certainly contributed our share. Girls on all sides of us were saying, "Isn't he adorable!" "He's so handsome!" "What a wonderful smile!" We looked around at them, pleased they agreed with us, but we felt a bit superior because we had gotten his autograph.

So I, who had never cared about the game, was captivated by football. We could sometimes, by hook or by crook, get hold of a newspaper that printed news of the Crimson Tide, but not until Uncle Joe bought us that Silvertone radio could we listen to the games. And we listened to every game no matter how harrowing. The excited voice of the announcer, the glad exclamations of greetings in the background, all the hurly-burly of a game day made us feel as though we were there ourselves.

In 1937 the Georgia Tech and Alabama faced off in Birmingham. We listened to the "inquiring mike" program originating from the Thomas Jefferson Hotel. The announcer asked one man why he was in Birmingham. His answer: "I'm here to see Bama beat the hell out of Tech." The announcer then asked a girl if she thought Alabama would win. Her answer: "By gum, we'd better!" The hotel manager told the radioman that they had over 700 people in 350 rooms. Through Uncle Joe's radio we were there!

But the game didn't go as smoothly as these people expected. Tech outplayed Alabama in every way. Neither team scored until the last six minutes of the game when Alabama made a touchdown to keep clean her undefeated record. It was an afternoon of terror. Joe Kilgrow played the entire game. He had also played the previous Saturday against Tulane. I wished then that he would be invited to our school's football banquet later in the fall.

The game the Tide played on Thanksgiving Day was even more nerve-racking. The next day I wrote in my diary:

What a game that was yesterday! I can't even be flippant about it. Vanderbilt's line certainly earned that name "seven stalwart men."

*The score was Vandy 7, Bama 6 when Sanford was sent in to try
a field goal. I left the room. I couldn't stand the suspense. But the
kick was good! It was good! I thought I would faint. The game was
over in a few minutes.*

*The announcer said he took off his hat to whatever kind of toe
Sanford had on his right foot. So do I.*

In December I was one of the waitresses chosen to serve at Brookwood's football banquet. Nell and I asked our teacher, Mrs. Pruitt, to
let us serve the guest table. I didn't yet know who the guests would be
but I knew one or two of them would be from the Crimson Tide. They
were late arriving. Everyone had begun eating when I left the dining
room for the kitchen and met my dream—Joe Kilgrow and Heyward
Sanford.

I gasped, "Are you all from the university?"

They said, "Yes."

"Well . . . well, I mean, well, I'll take your coats."

Sanford handed me his hat and overcoat. I was reaching for Kilgrow's when Nell came up and said, "I'll take his."

Mrs. Pruitt appeared and said, "Yes, you'd better. Aileen can't take
both. I'll show them to their places."

Grrrr! I could have taken them both. I meant to take them both,
greedy soul that I was! How handsome they were in outfits that looked
brand new and expensive. During the meal I served them first even
though the county superintendent of schools sat at the other end of
the table. I just knew I would spill coffee on them—I was so excited!

Hubert, a member of our school's senior class, was toastmaster. In
his introduction of the Tide players he said, "When we asked Sandy
Sanford out, as he is such a good kicker we thought we would ask him
to take off his shoe. As for Joe Kilgrow, he's such a great runner I guess
we'd better ask him to take off his pants." That made everybody laugh.

After we servers finished our work, we were allowed to sit together
near the kitchen door to watch what went on. I was all eyes.

Sanford talked more than Kilgrow. He was more outgoing. He gave
an exhibition of trucking, bending his arms at the elbows, pointing
to the ceiling, and waggling his index fingers as he "trucked" along.
Everybody was delighted. When he finished, Mr. Jones, our principal,

said, "I made a mistake a while ago when I said that was Sandy Sanford. I believe it was Joe E. Brown, from Hollywood." That brought
out another long laugh from the crowd as we all knew the comedian
with the grin stretching from ear to ear. I thought Sanford's grin was
attractive, not funny.

When they left the table, I rushed over to get their place cards for
souvenirs. I pocketed Sanford's but Kilgrow took his with him. Then
I joined the crowd around them hoping for an autograph. After getting Kilgrow's, I backed out to breathe, then squeezed into the crowd
for Sanford's. After signing my program, he said, "Here, Joe, sign
this," and handed the program to Kilgrow. So I accidentally got two of
Kilgrow's!

Nell and I shook their hands and told them we'd be listening when
they played in the Rose Bowl and we hoped they'd win. They both
smiled and said, "Thank you." Reluctantly we left them, clutching our
precious programs, and went to sit in the servers' chairs.

"Wasn't Joe's hand soft?" Nell marveled. "Isn't he the cutest thing?" We
were used to shaking hands with men who cut cordwood, or worked in
sawmills, or held on to a plow that was turning up new ground.

"They probably get manicures at the beauty shop," I whispered.

Now the dancing began. Most of us were Baptist and didn't dance,
not because we didn't want to, but because we didn't know how and
our church disapproved. Sitting on the sidelines, we watched the
laughing, dancing couples, envious of every girl the Tiders danced
with. Some of them did the Big Apple, the famous dance we had all
heard about but had never seen danced.

They went at it tooth and nail—what energy and noise. Any one of
us would have risked being called up before the church next day and
reprimanded just for the chance of being a part of all that exuberance.

My diary entry for January 1, 1938, gave little space to the Rose
Bowl, lost by Alabama 13–0: "Woe, woe—sob, sob—I sit broken-
hearted amid the ruins of a Rose Bowl dream. But Auburn won, thank
goodness. Bama needed Auburn's Spec Kelly in the Rose Bowl . . ."

My football fever lasted only a short time until I had to go to work
to earn a living, and the problems of the adult world took all my time
and strength.

26

A Movie Star Thrill

I WAS IN THE TWELFTH grade in 1938 when I saw in the newspaper at school that the famous singing movie star Nelson Eddy was to appear in Birmingham. I yearned to go with all my heart but I lived in the red clay hills of Tuscaloosa County. What chance did I have? Then an amazing thing happened. The Frisco Railroad called Daddy to work third trick at Freight Yard Junction in Birmingham that night. And Daddy said he'd take me! I had forty-nine cents from typing for my teacher's husband. Daddy gave me a penny to make enough for a gallery ticket. In my diary I wrote: "March 3, 1938: I spent most of the few minutes after I found I could go collecting my overcoat, our lunch, a scarf, and everything else I thought I'd need. All the way to Birmingham I was haunted by the dread there would be no gallery tickets left. The old lizzie crawled along so slowly and every car that zoomed past I'd say to myself, 'They're sho' going.'"

At last I got my first look at Birmingham. Daddy showed me Vulcan standing on the mountain way, way across town. At the Tutwiler Hotel I was so busy looking around that I didn't notice where we were going. The little look-see I had was interesting! The man at the desk said the box office had been moved to the auditorium at five that afternoon. He told us how to get there and sent us out a side door. He said that was so we wouldn't lose our bearings, but maybe he wanted us to disappear quick as we certainly didn't fit in that glamorous setting.

When we had come in the front, the revolving door had been moving so I thought it went automatically. When I stepped into the door on the way out, I started moving but the door stood still. I got a crack on my noggin that made me understand I was supposed to push, and I did. We had to walk two or three blocks back to the car and then try to find the Municipal Auditorium. We got caught in two or three traffic jams and finally stopped at a gas station to ask for directions. The attendant said we'd passed it. We tried to turn around and go back. Several cars got crossed and it seemed ages until we arrived at the place. I was a knot of anxiety but Daddy never once lost patience.

There were crowds all out in front. Another age passed before we found a parking place and then Daddy had to drive in several times before he had the lizzie fixed right. We walked three blocks back to the Aud and went inside. I looked around at all those young men in tuxedoes and the women in evening gowns. We finally found a line in front of the ticket window. After standing there for fifteen minutes, inching up to the window, the woman said, "Gallery tickets outside around the corner." When we got around there, we had to stand in another line, but I finally clutched the green ticket in my hand. Daddy left to go to work and I scooted up about fifteen flights of stairs, presented my ticket at the door, and began searching for a seat. I had begun to think I wouldn't find one but in the very last row there were several. All the while before the show started I watched the young ladies (old ladies too) below (miles below!) flirting around in their long, slinky evening gowns.

The main lights went off and the spotlight focused on the piano. Everybody started clapping and in a few minutes Nelson Eddy himself strode out on the stage. I was very disappointed because I couldn't distinguish a single feature of his face. I could tell he was blond and could see his figure distinctly but not his face. Most of his selections were operatic. I enjoyed "The Blind Ploughman" and, as an encore, "Sweetheart, Will You Remember." I liked that one best of all. He sang it last and everybody was humming it as we left. I also remember a song about a king wearing purple tights (ha, ha, ha, ha, ha), and another Monsieur Eddy said was about a French soldier who returned home to find that his sweetheart had married another man, and he was "quite put out about it."

When it was over (it seemed mighty short for fifty cents), I strolled into the bottom part of the auditorium and looked around. I found a program on the floor, and tucking it under my arm, I dashed up the street keeping an eye out for Daddy. He was standing on the corner and we went to the lizzie.

In a few minutes I got my first look at Freight Yard Junction. It was a gray building, little and long, and on the inside the dust was two inches thick. The second-trick operator said MacBride, the agent, swept the inside once a month and sprinkled water on the old wood floor to keep the dust from choking him.

Soon after we got there, I went out to the car and crawled under the overcoats on the back seat. About eleven o'clock I went back in the office and stayed until one or two o'clock. Then I went out and slept in the car until I nearly froze and then went back inside the building. I listened to the dispatcher's phone and slept awhile on the table, until the telegraph instruments woke me, then I crawled back in the car again. The car was parked between two railroad tracks, and if there was not a train going by on one, rooting, tooting, bong-bonging, spew-spewing, racket-racketing, there was a train on the other. And when they were not there, the planing mill next door was letting off steam. At six o'clock I ate a dried beef and lettuce sandwich. Mmmmmmmgood. Agent MacBride came in at seven thirty and we left about an hour later.

27

Magic at the New Bama Theatre

MAMA AND I, IN TUSCALOOSA one day in spring 1938, made our simple purchases and then were free until Daddy got off from work to take us home. As we came out of the store, I announced, "We're finished. Now, let's go to the show!"

I was wild to see the movies, and I had read about the wonderful new Bama Theatre. I *had* to see it. Of course, the admission price was prohibitive—now that I was sixteen I was considered an adult and had to pay thirty cents. I had held on to sixty cents from the typing I did for my teacher's husband, and it was burning a hole in my pocket.

"I think not," Mama said. "There's no sense spending money with nothing to show for it."

"But you'll see Clark Gable and Myrna Loy," I insisted. "It's *Test Pilot* and has lots of airplanes and things."

"I see all the airplanes I want to flying over the house every day," she said.

"Oh but, Mama, the new theater is more than just a movie theater!" I protested. "Didn't you read about it in the paper? The main floor is a beautiful Spanish garden, and the ceiling is full of lighted stars twinkling in a dark sky." I took a deep breath. "And—and the article said that misty clouds drift overhead, and you're transported to a paradise." I knew the details by heart but added some of my own.

She couldn't understand what a world of magic was waiting for us. Daddy wouldn't get off from work until five. Here was *my* chance and I couldn't miss it. I gave Mama three dimes from the six I clutched in my hand, and she set out for J. C. Penney to buy things she needed. I went in the opposite direction, headed for the corner of Sixth Street and Greensboro Avenue. As I loped past the big clock near Tuscaloosa's one skyscraper, the ten-story First National Bank on Main Street, I noticed its hour hand pointed to one. I'd be just in time for the first show.

I approached the building almost on tiptoe. A little depot standing alone out front with a girl inside must be the ticket place, I decided, so I laid down my three dimes. The girl punched a button and a ticket shot out. I took it and turned to face a vast frontage of shining glass and chrome.

Where was the door?

I could not find it. I hung around hoping someone would come along and go in ahead of me, or else come out, so I could know which of those many glassed wall areas was the entrance. I was determined not to let anyone guess that I was the country bumpkin that I really was. Finally, I noticed a man in a white uniform standing inside. I pushed on the glass panel nearest him, and it opened. The gold-braided man held out his hand, and I gave him my ticket. Then, I stepped into the lobby and found myself confronted on every side with more doors. None of them had signs.

With false self-assurance (in case someone was watching), I headed for the nearest one. It opened on a stairway. I went up three flights, finding elegance on every landing—large, gold-framed mirrors, soft pillowed sofas, graceful chairs, and what looked like real paintings. I almost bogged down in the deep carpets, all in rich colors. Everything was so imposing, so grand. I felt overwhelmed.

I heard typewriter keys clacking so I knew this third floor must be the business part of the theater. I turned a corner and entered a long, wide hall with more elegant chairs, divans, mirrors, lighted lamps, and paintings. The deep noiseless rugs almost tripped me. Everywhere I looked there was so much beauty and luxury. I felt I was walking through the pages of the *House Beautiful* magazines Aunt Clara brought us.

Music drifted around me. Following the sound, I located steps that led up. I had found the balcony. For a minute I admired the sky—yes, the stars looked as real as the Brookwood stars—but something was happening on-screen so I crept down the dark aisle to a seat in the front row.

Right away, I was dissatisfied, not liking that I had to look down at the picture, but the news reel had begun before I got up the courage to leave and take up my search again for the Spanish garden.

I lit out down the hall in what I thought would be the right direction, peeking in every door I passed. The beautiful women's lounge invited me in, but I didn't have time to investigate—I could hear talking now. The main show was on!

Farther down the hall and up some more steps and here I was in the balcony again. By now I was so desperate I would have asked for directions, country bumpkin or not, but in all of these nooks and crannies, not another soul crossed my path. I came back in the hall and went in what I thought was the opposite direction from the one I'd been going. With a sigh of relief, I found the steps down to the lobby, and following the sound of airplane motors, I arrived in the Spanish garden. I could see twining vines and big blossoms and what looked like fruit. The sky was much prettier from there. I studied it but couldn't discover how the clouds rolled back and forth. At the same time, I was also watching Myrna Loy and Clark Gable emoting on-screen.

But when Spencer Tracy appeared, my attention was totally his. I thought Loy was lovely, Gable handsome, but Tracy was marvelous as Gunnar the gum-chewing mechanic with his look of such kindness. I forgot how hard I had struggled to find them, and I was in the story with them.

At five, bewitched and dazed, I came out into the daylight of Tuscaloosa more determined than ever to force my parents to share this magical world. I met Mama in the lobby of the McLester Hotel. She had spent her thirty cents for a remnant, a pretty red fabric sprinkled with white flowerets, enough to make a skirt for one of us girls or to line a quilt.

During the following weeks, I renewed my nagging. I stressed the wonders of the Spanish garden and the sky that shone with stars.

Daddy said, "Gee, I sure would like to see that sky."

Finally, Mama agreed to go. I carefully studied the film schedule. I wanted something to make them laugh, to forget the Great Depression that they dealt with every day. That's why I turned down *Boys' Town,* even though Spencer Tracy was in it. I was afraid it would be sad.

Finally, I picked *Alexander's Ragtime Band.* During the show, I kept glancing at them to see how they were reacting but in the flickering light I could only see them staring straight ahead.

At the end of the movie, as we made our way toward the door, Mama said, "We'd better hurry to the grocery store before it closes."

Daddy had to count what money he had so we'd know how much we could buy. It took a lot of thought and consultation to fit our food needs to our funds. When we finished loading our purchases, dark was coming and we had to hurry home to take care of the night work. We had no time to talk about the show until we sat down for supper.

"Well, how did you all like the movie?" I asked.

Mama said, "That music was too loud—it deafened me."

Daddy said, "Gee whiz, Aileen. I forgot to look up at the sky."

Taken aback, I could only say, "Well, that means we have to go again, doesn't it?"

They gazed down at their cornbread and buttermilk and said nothing. Yet I understood.

They didn't want to hurt my feelings, but they could not be a part of my magic, make-believe world. They could not share it. But I saw a flash of something more, something that saddened me to tears: my parents, who had guided me, shielded me, educated me, and kept me alive, were lagging behind. They could not free themselves from the dreary present, while I was eager, yet fearful, for the future.

We never mentioned the theater again.

Afterword

THESE STORIES END WITH THE late 1930s but the Great Depression continued. As we children grew older, we found jobs, always low-paying, and could help the family a bit. As World War II came closer, more jobs opened up, especially for women. Gradually, the wolf faded away from our door, but for the rest of our lives we feared he might, like the Howton Horror, come back at any moment to hold us hostage once again.